Impossible Is Where Logical Thinking
Ends and Creative Thinking Begins

This Book Is Dedicated To
Savo Bojicic
Inventor Of The Original Think Tank

Published by: Wayne Russell
Website: https://lateralthinkingcousre.com
Email: support@lateralthinkingcourse.com

Preface………………………………………………... 1

Introduction…………………………………….… 2

Imagination……………………………………….… 6

The Brain……………………………………… 11

Hundred Billion Dollar Accident……………………. 14

Ninety Billion Idle Neurons…………………………. 16

2.4 Million Years For A Handle……………………. 19

Steam Slept Through The Ages Out In Plain View.. 22

Today Is 50,000 Years Too Late…..………………. 24

The Power Of "Why"………………………………. 28

Let Us Change……………………………............. 31

How Good Is Your Mind………………………….... 34

Test Your Mind…………………………………... 39

Activity #1- The Penny……………………………. 39

Activity #2- "Why"…………………………………. 41

Activity #3- "Toothpick"…………………………. 43

Activity #4- "Line"………………………………... 44

Activity #5- Two Circles……………………………. 45

Activity #6- "Rope Belt"………………………………… 46

Activity #7- "Door"………………………………… 47

Activity #8- "Two Strings"……………………………… 48

Activity #9- "1+1"……………………………….. 49

Activity #10- "ZERO"………………………………… 51

A New Way To Think……………………………….. 52

Two Stages Of Thinking………………………….. 57

Logical Thinking………………………………… 62

Two Types Of Imagination…………………............ 66

Impossible Does Not Mean Impossible…………… 69

Use Of Random or Chance Inputs………………… 73

Challenge Established Concepts…………………… 74

Association Of Ideas…………………………… 82

Free Associations By A Word……………………… 89

Free Associations Exercises…………….............. 91

Random Word Use For RES Technique…………… 92

How Random Words Work………………………… 100

FAQ……………………………………………… 106

What Is A Word... 109

More FAQ's.. 111

Be Clear About The Problem............................. 113

PREFACE

Impossible... what a powerful word. It will stop one man in his tracks or inspire a nation to greatness. If you were to dig deep enough into the history of almost everything Mankind has accomplished, from our morning cup of coffee to putting a man on the moon, you will likely find it was met with many "impossibles" by the naysayers and critics of the day. Yet, history has built and continues to build mountain ranges of debunked "impossibles".

Famous are those history changing impossible defying events like the Wright brothers' first flight or John F. Kennedy's proclamation: "*we will put a man on the moon within 10 years*". Both were mocked and scoffed at by the so called "experts" of the time.

Every day far less but equally proclaimed "impossibles" fall and are tossed on top of the heap by those creative individuals who dare challenge the world, pursue their ambitions, and chase relentlessly what they believe is possible.

Creative people prefer the challenges of life over the guaranteed existence of Mediocrity.

This guide is not about the positive "self talk" touted by endless armies of motivational speakers, although I absolutely subscribe to enlivening the "power of the mind" through positive thought.

This guide *is* about giving you a proven technique called "REST" (Random External Stimulus Technique) to develop and train your creative thinking mind by looking at problems from a totally different reference point to uncover solutions that were previously hidden or considered "impossible".

INTRODUCTION

Imagine that you have ten million dollars locked in a safe. It has been so long since you opened that safe you can no longer remember the combination. The safe is just sitting inaccessible, dormant with its contents totally unproductive and useless to you.

The world we live in demands new ideas. It craves for new things, new ways to improve, build, transport, distribute, house, feed, grow, play, communicate, look, and live.

The world's appetite for new things is insatiable.

There has never been a time in history where so many people have so many opportunities to change their situation and bring abundance into their lives.

The answer to every question is locked away in the safe of your subconscious, if only you possessed the combination which opens the door. Think about this for a minute. The average human brain has a capacity to store 20 billion bits of information. Yet, in an entire lifetime of memories no human on earth has stored even one million bits of information or one part in twenty thousand!

This *Definitive Guide to Solving the Impossible* teaches the Random External Stimulus Technique, (REST) which holds the combination to open the safe. When you master the process of REST, which will later become clear and familiar to you, everything will change!

With this guide and practice you gain access to treasures buried deep within your mind, allowing you to develop your true potential for success, fulfillment, and ultimate happiness.

This is much more than just solving puzzles, although solving puzzles is the pathway to getting started. Practice makes perfect, so having fun while training your mind to "think outside the box" makes the journey all that more entertaining.

Training the mind on a new way of thinking is the goal of using REST. When logic fails to provide the answers you require, you will now have a system to follow that will flood your mind with new ideas for logic to pursue.

The material presented here is easy to use. It provides many challenges as well as good clean fun. I hope you enjoy the process of change you are about to enter and forever benefit from the experience.

Just as we benefit from exercising our bodies, exercising our minds brings tremendous advantages. When you engage in exercise to gain physical strength you feel better, have more energy, sleep peacefully and enjoy an overall sense of well being. Jogging, Cycling and Aerobics are but a sampling of activities you can use to build physical strength.

Exercising your mind is no different. When you engage in activities that build mind power you feel better, energize your mind, sleep well and acquire an overall sense of inner peace.

Building mind power should be fun, for it is the road to learning new things, something you are never too old to stop doing.

I have spent countless hours researching and by chance discovered this unique method, which helped me, and I believe will help you multiply the power of your mind.

You will acquire a new and unexpected mental supremacy, new fluency of ideas, and new ways of looking at everything you see, learn, and do. Regardless how much education you have attained, the material presented here will benefit you immensely. It is like having your own personal trainer 24/7.

The more you use this technique, the more convinced you will be about its tremendous power. In fact, REST is a generator of new ideas.

To think creatively requires you have an original thought, one you had not thought of before. However, this is easier said than done.

Let's think of the power contained in the English Alphabet. With just 26 simple, oddly shaped lines, we can describe everything that is or ever was and everything that will ever be.

These 26 simple scribbles have put men on the moon, transplanted hearts, built massive structures, moved mountains, created works of art, pierced into the deep remote depths of oceans, viewed the most distant points of the known universe, save endangered species, started and ended wars, produced new countries and destroyed others.

Simply by arranging these 26 symbols into an endless combination of *patterns* we can accomplish anything.

The mind thinks in patterns, mostly "instinctive" patterns which have formed over a million years of evolution. Our survival instinct is engaged constantly; it is what drives us to go out each day to earn a living, allowing us to acquire the necessities of life.

Our instinctive "fight or flight" pattern is engaged at various degrees of intensity when we are confronted with situations that threaten us physically or mentally.

Our instinctive behaviours are only slightly modified by our experiences since birth, which make each one of us unique.

Our patterns of thought work at both the conscious and subconscious levels. Most people go through life giving little or no thought to their instinctive behaviour and the powerful influence it has on their day-to-day activities. For the purpose of developing your creativity, we will not be discussing the instinctive patterns of thought we all have. However, understanding them will explain much about the effects our instincts have on our daily lives.

By eliminating our self-destructive patterns of thought we build new productive patterns. As your mind power increases your creative thinking faculties explode!

The process of finding new patterns of thought is called "Lateral Thinking". A principle theorized by Dr. Edward de Bono. Lateral Thinking is to creative thinking as carbon is to life. It is required in order to forge new patterns of thought, which are core to any real effort of creative thinking.

Lateral Thinking, in a way, is like the A-B-C's of the alphabet: it is powerful, imaginative, instructional, and educational. Lateral Thinking taps into the imaginative subconscious mind where "infinite intelligence" resides. It helps you break down the barriers and limitations that a lifetime of using logic has built and unlocks the unlimited potential of your mind.

IMAGINATION

Great ideas do not come by themselves; they incubate in the creative faculties of the mind. There are two types of creative thinking processes we use: synthetic imagination and the creative imagination.

Synthetic imagination is engaged when we can improve upon a known idea, position two or more known ideas together in an unusual way, or use an existing idea for totally different and innovative application.

Creative imagination is engaged when we come up with a totally new and revolutionary idea that is original.

There is little difference between a genius and the average person. It is the development and mastery of a powerful imagination that creates a genius. Genius requires the use of imagination to create results that no one has thought of previously. It is peculiar though, how most great ideas, once known, become obvious. One wonders why they had not been thought of before.

Random External Stimulus Technique (REST) directs you out of the well-established patterns thought and into new patterns that stimulate the imagination and creative thinking processes of the mind. It's powerful because you are directed toward strange, unfamiliar and unpredictable territory.

Solving puzzles is fun entertainment but learning a process of "how to" solve puzzles or "puzzling problems" is of much greater benefit to you and the world around you! This is how new ideas emerge from a well-trained mind.

Solving Puzzles that can not be solved using logic are not only fun, they can truly change your life!

New ideas do not have to be something made of steel,

plastic, wood, or cloth. A new idea could be a new way of doing something, a service, a better way of changing or improving an existing item, even a new outlook on life and how to live.

A new idea does not have to be big. It could be a part of your day-to-day activity, a new way to break a bad habit, a new approach to a relationship, a new "twist" to induce your child to eat their broccoli.

There is no limit to the need for new and original ideas!

REST is not a time-consuming exercise. If you practise it only a few minutes every day, the results will astonish you. New ideas come in a flash, ignited by a sudden inspiration from an unexpected source when randomly presented.

REST is a tool, and like any tool, you should use it according to its function. You cannot very well drill a hole with a measuring tape. You cannot trim your hair with a lawn mower. You cannot go faster by whipping a motorcycle or filling up a horse with gasoline.

Lateral Thinking using REST is habit-forming, like anything that is fun and entertains. The more you practise it, the more value you will get out of it. You will condition your mind to associate objects and ideas automatically without effort; your subconscious will be engaged more often by learning and mastering this technique.

This method is not repetitive, boring, or trivial. It is always interesting, always stimulating, always new. It may spark a revolutionary "life changing" idea or a faster way to advance your career. It may help you to be successful beyond your wildest dreams.

This guide is unique. I have assembled the materials presented here from a wide and exhaustive variety of sources. Until now they only existed scattered in bits and pieces.

My hope for this guide is to be of great benefit to you. If it is to be of great value, the information must be beneficial; it is indispensable for the thorough understanding of REST.

This guide has an open end, and you should come back to it often to clarify certain points or to exercise novel ideas. It will serve as a refresher for your day-to-day work.

Keeping in mind above observations, I designed this guide with the following objectives in mind:

I. To make you aware of the importance acquiring a solid creative thinking skill has for solving Life's "Greatest Puzzles", whether it be in business, profession, social and political pursuits, family life, self-improvement or just some good old fashion fun.

2. To show you that your mind has a tremendous power, it only lacks development and usage of that which it is capable of; the power of any decent mind can be multiplied many folds.

3. To show you that no idea is so outlandish that you should not consider it.

4. To help you broaden your horizons, place you above average humans and become an exceptional individual.

5. To acquire a strong habit for association of ideas involving both concrete and abstract meanings.

6. To convince you that the Random External Stimulus Technique is powerful, rewarding, and indispensable. This guide shows you how to harness the amazing power of REST for new ideas.

7. To explain how and why REST works, and how it can be an indispensable "idea machine" for the enrichment of your life.

8. To help you find brilliant solutions to all your puzzles in life, no matter how big or how small they might be.

9. To prove that creative, inventive, and imaginative thinking is not a special gift, the privilege of only a few, but a skill that anyone with a decent mind can learn and retain for life.

10. Not to accept the obviousness of an idea, but to challenge it, no matter how evident its value seems. There are always better ideas waiting to replace the old ones.

11. Occasionally, suspend logical thinking in favour of non-logical thinking that could lead you to new, original, and

unexpected results.

12. To become a genius or near-genius, and shine amongst your peers.

THE BRAIN

You possess the most powerful instrument in the known universe— your brain! It is the central exchange of all information transmitted by our senses and distributed throughout your entire body.

It correlates communications; it originates responses, stores impressions, and lastly becomes the seat of your intelligence. Your brain works by electrical and chemical impulses transmitted through nerve cells called neurons.

Your brain contains 100 billion of these neurons. Their capacity is so vast that they could absorb the entire knowledge created by mankind since its beginning. The capacity of your brain is so huge that it can hold much, much more than it holds from an entire lifetime of experiences.

During your life, you may receive a trillion bits of information. Only a very small number of these enter your conscious memory. The majority of them are dormant, inactive, and end up in your subconscious. They may seem to have been completely discarded until something triggers their memory.

We receive daily about one hundred thousand sensory

inputs. Everything you hear, touch, smell, taste, and see every moment, your mind processes and interprets. Your brain stores every detail of your daily activities. Most of these details enter your brain without your conscious knowledge. Their interpretation and filing into your subconscious is instantaneous, faster than the speed of your conscious awareness. And it is good fortune our brain — this incredible machine — functions in such a way, allowing us tostore the flood of daily information we receive into the subconscious part of the mind; otherwise, we would all go insane.

Scientists estimate that the average human brain has a capacity of 20 billion bits of information. When you consider that a maximum of one million of them are stored in the brain during a lifetime, the actual size of available untapped brain power is an incredible twenty thousand times more!

Another interesting fact is that the average human brain interconnects all neurons in 1,000,000,000,000 (one thousand trillion) ways! There is certainly no danger that you will overload your brain. The nature of the brain is such that it has more power than simply processing our five sensory inputs; as a race we are only just scratching the surface of what our minds can accomplish.

Science has already proven the power of the mind can cross vast distances and "see" through walls. Law enforcement agencies and the military employ people all the time with well developed "clairvoyant" abilities to find victims or "see" what the enemy is doing.

The mechanism of the human brain is so complex. The most sophisticated computer, compared to the brain, is a very crude machine. Comparing our mind to a computer would be like comparing the most intricate machinery of today to the chipping tools of the primitive humans of 500,000 years ago.

In a computer, massive amounts of information are stored for almost instantaneous retrieval, but only after a human programmer has implanted programs and data into its memory chips. We can only retrieve the data, which has been previously programmed into it.

There are cutting edge computers with the ability to crudely learn from the environment around them and adjust its behaviour accordingly. For now, the majority are completely oblivious to anything other than what has been programmed into it. A computer cannot reason, feel, love, imagine, cry, or laugh. It is simply not human — it is only a tool.

It is an increasingly sophisticated, tireless machine whose function is to make more efficient our quest to acquire knowledge of the universe and to live more comfortable, productive lives.

The human brain functions differently than a computer. Imagine a library where a proper registration and classification system of all the books does not exist.

The readers would return the books and place them anywhere on any shelf. Library visitors would not be able to retrieve their desired book and the library would be non-functional.

Imagine the information perceived by your brain; it is stored mostly as the returned books in this fictional library.

How then does the brain retrieve specific information? How does it sort out instantly any data, regardless of the time and place that such data was recorded? How can the brain recognize the desired information? How can it process all information almost instantly? How can it combine various details disregarding any filing system known to humans? How can it add colour, taste and form to any given set of facts? How can it use its power of locomotion called imagination, faster than the speed of light? How can it cross the barriers of time and space with ease?

How the brain does all these things is still a mystery. Its prodigious ability is the basis of the REST.

Without this ability, the brain could not function. With it, REST becomes an awesome power tool at your disposal.

Learn to use it creatively, intelligently, and wisely.

HUNDRED BILLION DOLLAR ACCIDENT

Most advancements, if not all, have at some point been stimulated by chance or accident. In medicine, for example, the incident of accidental discoveries is so high that there is hardly any major breakthrough, which did not happen by accident.

One of the earliest accidental discoveries is fire. Without fire, mankind would have surely perished. Our earth would have been inhabited by all other living creatures, but not humans.

The most famous accidental discovery occurred in the laboratory of British researcher and scientist Sir Alexander Fleming. As a young doctor, during the First World War, he saw many soldiers dying from superficial wounds because of infection and gangrene. At that time, he made a vow to devote his entire life work to the search of an agent he called "the magic bullet," capable of arresting infections.

He worked on this project day and night in his laboratory, for more than 20 years, without any notable success. One day, he put a sample of one of his experiments with microbes, on the sill of an open window.

"By chance", the wind blew something from the neighbouring trees into his microbe container. When he approached the windowsill to check the damage to his experiment, he was surprised at first, then awestruck.

He found that all microbes were dead. As he rushed to his microscope to examine what happened, a great elation overtook him; he realized that he finally had in his grasp the "magic bullet", which had eluded him for so many years.

Here at last, by a miraculous accident, was the answer to his long search. After careful analysis, he discovered that what fell on his sample was a fungus called penicillium notatum.

This was a monumental historical accident. This discovery was in fact, Penicillin. This "accident" produced sales, in excess of 100 billion dollars worldwide. Penicillin gave birth to many potent derivatives, which increase this monetary sum to an amount of many more billions of dollars.

More than money, penicillin provided incalculable benefits to all mankind.

We may ask ourselves why it is so difficult to come up with revolutionary ideas and discoveries. Why were we unable to generate brilliant solutions to many of our problems, when our minds possess such a huge capacity?

Why do we have to wait for chance and lucky accidents?

We don't...

NINETY BILLION IDLE NEURONS

Most psychologists agree that we use no more than 10 percent of the capacity of our brains. The average brain, the instrument of the mind, contains 100 billion brain cells called neurons. It is estimated that 90 billion brain cells are simply idle. The 10 percent that we do use include the biological functions for the vast control of the entire human organism.

Can you imagine a business that works on just 10 percent of its capacity? Such a business would go bankrupt in a very short time. How would you feel if you received only 10 cents of every dollar you earned? What if your heart worked at only 10 percent of its capacity? You would not live very long; you would not be alive to read this guide. If the sun produced only 10 percent of its current capacity, what would happen to our planet and everything on it? It would freeze to such a low temperature that nothing and nobody could live on it.

Extensive new studies about the human mind prove that its power is far greater than anyone has anticipated.

It is a strange fact that our entire educational system ignores this capacity of the human mind. Every educator is well aware of the high degree of imagination exhibited by young children. Their minds, although not fully developed, are highly creative. They conceive original ideas constantly but are often encouraged to stop being silly or day dreaming.

What happened to our highly imaginative capacity?

Sadly, "snap out of it" or "wake up and pay attention" are just a few favourite lessons constantly drilled into our young.

Unfortunately, the present education system gradually and systematically suppresses our creativity. This organized suppression starts the day we are born. Most parents unwittingly teach their children to abandon their creative abilities when implanting the first seeds of proper behaviour. "No" is most often the first word a child learns the meaning of.

The educational system completes the abandonment of our creativity with a curriculum of facts and logic. Not that facts and logic are not important - they are. But imagination is thought as a waste of time and not given the credit it deserves.

I remember when I was a child. My class was painting with different objects. I used an onion cut in half to paint mine. I would dip the cut portion in green paint and stamp a print of it over and over on a large Bristol board. At the last minute, for whatever reason, I mixed the colour red in with the green and made one imprint of the onion in this new purplish colour.

When it came time to show our creations, my teacher was disappointed that I had changed the colour on the onion for only one impression. She thought my art was ruined because of it.

It is experiences like this that can cause a child to abandon their imagination or at least keep it to themselves or risk ridicule. A child becomes less imaginative and less inquisitive as they grow older finding it more desirable to "fit in". We instruct our children to conform and apply well established ways of behaviour, until the last creative flame is blown out and extinguished from their mind.

Our educational institutions do nothing to resuscitate the

imagination of our children. Rather we are taught the proper way (the logical way) to do something then go out and do it for pay.

We all are the products of this system. However, this guide is designed to teach you how to rediscover and ignite yourself, your mind, your imagination, and your intuition.

With the help of this guide you will employ more of your brain neurons; get them out of the unemployment line into active, beneficial, and productive service.

2.4 MILLION YEARS FOR A HANDLE

One of the principal differences between animals and humans is that humans can reason. We can logically deduce and employ our imagination to discover how to use and improve tools for our benefit.

The use of simple tools dates to about 2,400,000 years BC when various shaped stones were used to strike wood, bone, or other stones to break them apart and shape them.

Stones attached to sticks with strips of leather or animal sinew were being used as hammers by about 30,000 years BC during the middle of the Palaeolithic Stone age.

What was so strange about this?

The fact, verified by anthropologists, that these chipping tools were in use at least 2,400,000 years ago and went unchanged for 2,370,000 years! Then about 30,000 years BC there was a notable improvement or technological advancement, the addition of a handle.

Human progress was painfully slow. By about 5,000 years ago, the rate of change in human development had quickened substantially.

What happened to human development from 2.4 million years ago to 30,000 years ago? We know that the quality of human intelligence reached a point comparable to current times about 200,000 years ago, possibly much earlier.

The average size of human brain 200,000 years ago was about 1300 CC, same as the average human brain of today.

The fact it took 2,370,000 years for those early humans just to add a handle to their tools testifies to our slow and agonizing advancement, a fact, that best reveals the excruciating tardiness of human creativity.

The quality and capacity of early human brains, hundreds of thousands of years ago is as good as ours is today. They had the same potential to think as we do now. Why then were they unable to accelerate their development much faster?

The only logical explanation is that early humans, like our ancestral monkeys, *instinctively* copied what they saw others do. Any advancement was discovered purely by accident.

Early man, perhaps out of necessity, were so consumed by surviving the day, no creative thought was given about how to improve their results tomorrow. An instinctive behaviour that unfortunately is still alive and well today in most people.

Despite tremendous advancements in the last one hundred years, most people still do not think for themselves. Most people follow, unconsciously, the "monkey see monkey do" behaviour, even though there has never been a better time in history than now for the individual to create the life of his/her dreams.

If only we would have the courage, chance being ridiculed, get creative and take action!

Most people ignore, or more accurately, bury their creative thinking capacity. We struggle with tremendous difficulties every day, yet do very little to discover or generate new ideas to solve them. The capacity of human intelligence is such that every average adult could approach the level of a genius, if he or she would dare to develop and use their minds in a more productive way.

If only they would change the way they think!

This guide and REST are the best tools currently available to help you become a new, creative thinker.

STEAM SLEPT THROUGH THE AGES

You often hear people talk about the fantastic technological advances modern man has achieved. Most people can tell you about many revolutionary discoveries and ideas. They can preach about enormous strides made in physics, applied sciences, and arts. Brag how the human genius triumphed and grew into the present state of civilization.

The truth is significant strides occurred only in the last 150 years with the arrival of the Industrial Revolution.

The big question is why the same Industrial Revolution did not occur 30,000 or 100,000 years ago?

Everything humans needed, all the raw materials required, existed on this planet millions of years ago. The Industrial Revolution of the mid-nineteenth century could have and should have occurred much, much earlier in human history.

Consider steam, for example. What is steam? It is power, an energy produced by the combination of the two oldest elements on earth, fire and water. Humans were agonizingly slow in harnessing this source of power, despite the fact, many such sources were on display all around them.

One of the major powers available to them was fire. In all probability, fire, like many other discoveries, happened by accident. Lightning had struck some dry leaves in the forest and caused a fire. The warmth and light from a fire to the early humans was certainly a mystery. Yet slowly, (and with a few burns I'm sure) they learned how to make and control fire at will.

The first harnessing of alternative power sources came much later after fire. Humans learned to harness animals to plough, lift water from canals for irrigation, thrash grain, run treadmills, and draw carts. Animals remained the chief source of mobile power until the invention of steam and gas engines.

Waterpower was available everywhere in nature. But we did not harness this abundant power until approximately 5,000 years ago when finally, the thought occurred to someone to use the river currents to lift water for irrigation.

The next notable use of waterpower occurred less than 200 years ago. The year was 1840 when water turbine came in use. Wind, another obvious power source now, has been around forever, but was not known to be employed by humans until about 3,000 B.C., when Egyptians added sails to their boats. Although wind power has been familiar since that time, early uses of the windmill, primarily for grinding and pumping wasn't used extensively until the late 12th century, and much later still for generating electrical power.

The economic use of steam as a source of power developed much later still.

Romans in the Middle Ages built toys that used steam. It did not occur to them that power could be used for industrial applications. Not until Watt's invention (1763 –1780's) did the steam engine convert that energy into motion.

Steam then became an important source of power that changed the world.

Theoretically, it was Sir Isaac Newton in England, in 1680 who invented the steam engine. His invention waited one hundred years to be usefully employed. The thinkers of the time were mentally blind not to see the tremendous value in steam as a source of energy. Steam, this ingenious power, which is so obvious to us today, lay dormant throughout the history of this planet waiting for someone to give some creative thought to the possibilities steam offers.

TODAY IS 199,746 YEARS TOO LATE

There is considerable controversy about the origins of humans and their dating. Most anthropologists agree, as a conservative estimate, the existence of humans on earth appeared one million years ago.

It took a further 700,000 years until humans reached a point classified as "homo sapiens" - the modern humans of today, as a distinctive species.

It has been determined 200,000 years ago, homo sapien's quality of human intelligence was as good as it is today. It is unbelievable that despite having had such excellent equipment at their disposal, humans were unable to advance as rapidly as they should have.

The basic inventions of fire, domestication of animals, and growing of food, did not occur until much later. The major changes came only after enormously long intervals of time.

The first period of rudimentary tools, simple forms of clothing and very basic shelters lasted for 170,000 years, more than three quarters of intelligent human existence. It took until the end of the Stone Age, the Neolithic Period about 12,000 years ago to add a series of fundamentals: Inventions for killing at a distance (bow and arrow), inventions for securing food at minimal effort, (traps and pits dug into the ground), inventions for exploiting food resources (plant cultivation, animal domestication), inventions for protection against elements (true clothing and constructed shelter), inventions of appliances for making artificial fabrics (weaving), for cooking (pottery) and for crossing waterways (canoes). All this took another span of 6,000 to 8,000 years more to be invented.

Consider, for example, another important invention — the screw. How old is the invention of the ordinary screw? It was unknown to the ancient civilizations. It was considered to be the product of Greek artisans at Alexandria in the 1st and 2nd century B.C.

Yet screw-like treads occur widely in nature, spiralling plants and vines for example, that hold a spiral "screw" like grip on each other. However, the possibility of creating something with similar spiralling treads for securing two parts together was not recognized until recent history.

It appeared for the first time in classic Mediterranean area where it was used in palm oil presses and in Roman surgical instruments for precise manipulation of their parts.

The real progress came quite late only about 150 years ago, when humans finally transitioned to a new era — the Industrial Revolution. Most machines, devices, and processes of modern times are merely massive improvements of elementary tools, devices, and processes inherited from ancient times.

Here are the main ones: abacus, axe, boat, bow and arrow, cart, chain, chisel, clothing, cog, wheel, cooking, digging, stick, fire, hammer, harness, hinge, irrigation, knife, lever, lock, money, needle, oar, pipe (water), plough, pottery, pulley, road, rope, rudder, sail, saw, screw, shovel, sled, time measuring devices, weaving, wedge and a yoke.

The abacus is the ancestor of the modern computer. The axe, the chisel, the knife, and the saw are used in modern cutting machines. All those inventions have their counterparts in ancient forms. The principle of their basic inventions exists in the most sophisticated machinery of today.

One of the earliest dreams of humans was to fly. Watching birds in the sky must have produced a strong desire to rise into the air. Yet humans thought it was impossible to glide through the air without falling back to the ground. That is until the laws of aerodynamics were understood.

If humans applied some creative effort to understand the principles of flight, they would have been able to fly 30,000 or 50,000 years ago! Certainly, all the materials necessary were at their disposal. Today the fascinating sport of "Hang Gliding" is well developed.

Humans finally found the way to fly using their own muscle power and the wind for lift and propulsion. All it took was some cloth (it could have easily been animal skins stretched thinly), some framing (made of cane, bamboo or light hardwood branches), and the knowledge of the flying principle.

The principles of flight, configured by mother nature and incorporated into the minds and wings of all birds, eluded humans.

A Frenchman, Jean Marie Le Bris, invented the first glider in 1855. He made a glide, an eighth of a mile long, in a boat-shaped machine patterned after the albatross!

For the record: All materials, all principles involved in every invention known and every invention to come has always been available at all times. Nothing on earth had to be imported from another planet by any individual or group. Even the most intricate piece of machinery of today existed, in its different forms, hundreds of thousands of years ago.

The Industrial Revolution, which started in mid-nineteen century, could have happened 50,000 years ago at least. The entire process of the development could have been shifted back in time, when the human brain reached the present standard of quality. Moreover, that was 300,000 years ago! We would be justified in being angry at our ancestors for not using their brainpower much earlier.

THE POWER OF WHY?

"Why" is the single most important question in life, asked by every person ever born. Young children pose this question more often than any other question. This question begs strongly for answers. It demonstrates the natural curiosity inherent in every human being.

So, let us ask a few whys.

Why is it difficult to produce new ideas?

The surprising answer: life exist in patterns. Fibonacci numbers, for example, are found everywhere in nature. These are set patterns or sequences of numbers that naturally occur in every living thing.

Why?

Because this is what makes life possible. If it were not so, humans would find it very difficult to get dressed in the morning, drive a car, go to work or go shopping. In all our activities, we follow the established patterns, and anticipate that our expectations will be fulfilled.

Why?

Because, for example, if you open a water faucet, you could hardly function if each time something different would flow out. When you talk into your phone, you would not expect your voice to become the musing sounds of a cow to the other person. By driving a car, you can hardly expect that it will suddenly turn on its side to get into a tight parking spot. However, new ideas are very opposite from the usual and expected patterns we live by. Ideas jump right out of the well-established patterns and present a new and unexpected view.

Why?

A mind that is conditioned to make the "strange" familiar is the very basis of learning. It cannot work in the opposite direction. It cannot conceive the "familiar" to be strange. That is the reason why the conditioned mind is so bad at producing new ideas. However, the mind is reasonably good at logical thinking.

Why?

Logic moves forward in a steady pattern, from step to step until a conclusion is reached. Unfortunately, new ideas involve strange steps that cannot be predicted. Computers are good at logic, but useless at producing new ideas.

Why?

Because we must program data into the computer so that

it can function. The computer can work usefully only after a human mind has programmed it. Only then can the computer function as a useful tool. However, the computer cannot create its own programming because it has no creative skills and it cannot think independently. Although new advancements in this area are being made, it can never advance to the same level as the human brain.

What is a new idea?

A new idea is something you have never heard of or seen before. It is an original thought for you. It is new because it is not familiar.

Why? Because you achieve innovation when, using imagination, you can take something that is familiar, and use it in an unfamiliar way. You innovate when you combine two or more familiar objects and create something unfamiliar or new. For example, water and fire are familiar. When we combine them we produce something new, steam.

By combining two familiar ideas, such as skis and a motorcycle, we create something new, the snowmobile. There is nothing new or surprising if you eat off of a plate made of plastic, because the plastic plate is a familiar object. However, when you use it in an unfamiliar way, such as throwing it upside down through the air, you create something new, a new invention - the Frisbee, a multi billion-dollar idea.

LET US CHANGE

You could start by first realizing that you already own outright, an instrument, which has unlimited capacity — your brain! Second, be convinced that something can be done, that new ideas do not come from someone who is smarter, possess a mystical gift or has magic powers. Third, understanding that there is no such thing as the "best" solution. Best ideas are only temporary until a better idea is found. Any idea at best is only "best for now" when we do not have a better one. A better idea is always there, lurking somewhere, waiting to be discovered by an alert mind.

From the previous chapters, you know that progress relied more on chance accidents during the entire period of human existence. In our past we accepted everything offered to us by nature with mere curiosity rather than a strong desire to understand, harness, improve, change, or innovate.

Looking back at recent centuries of human history, it is exceedingly difficult to accept and justify the slowness of our progress. We can only assume that humans had no ambition other than with their day-to-day living; they were complacent, as we are today. They were unwilling to change, unable to discover, hopelessly short of inventiveness, oblivious to their creative thinking abilities.

There is a valuable lesson to be learned from studying our past and current human behaviour. By examining our shortcomings, we can decide that old limiting beliefs shall not be repeated. Otherwise, what would be the purpose of learning about anything, history, archaeology, photography, anthropology, dancing, engineering, hockey, chemistry, chess, medicine, physics or sailing, for example?

Harold McMillan, former Prime Minister of United Kingdom, referring to the study of past human behaviour said, "We should consider the past as a springboard, not a sofa". Imagine for a moment that the ancient humans had discovered the principle of flying. If they had constructed a kind of flying machine and flown with it, say 100,000 years ego.

Where would we be today?

An interesting question, which would result in many intriguing answers!

Since you now realize the rate of change, in the past, has been so slow, you should be keenly aware the present rate of change has greatly accelerated.

This guide is your map of making a change with relatively little effort. The benefit will be with you for life.

You can change easily. Having a strong desire for a drastic change and the absolute belief that a change will benefit you will engage the awesome power of your mind. That power is in you, it is available for your use, and it is there in your head. You can access it at will, at all times, wherever you go.

Consider this statement "All humans want nowadays, is a womb with a view."

This quote, once quipped by Ashley Montague, demonstrates, in an unforgettable way, that the laziness of the present humans, who follow the line of least resistance, is not much different from that of their prehistoric ancestors.

Your mind is so powerful that you could do almost anything you wish.

Consider this: Your mind is able to accept, accomplish, activate, adapt, adopt, adorn, advance, advocate, affirm, build, break, create, correlate, combine, decide, dominate, discard, divide, eliminate, elevate, engineer, equalize, equate, examine, execute, expedite, extend, filter, focus, force, form, fuse, futurize, gather, generate, govern, gradate, grow, harmonize, harness, hold, humanize, hypnotize, idealize, identify, ideate, ignite, imagine, impose, improvise, improve, increase, induce, inflame, influence, initiate, innovate, integrate, intensify, interlock, invent, investigate, isolate, join, judge, juggle, jump, justify, know, lead, level, link, magnetize, make, manage, manoeuvre, master, match, measure, memorize, mend, monitor, monopolize, move, multiply, note, notify, observe, perate, optimize, organize, originate, overwhelm, penetrate, perceive, perform, persuade, position, pre-arrange, precipitate, predict,. prepare, pressure, produce, program, project, purify, quicken, quiz, rationalize, reason, recognize, refine, reform, regain, regulate, reinforce, replenish, reverse, revoke, rule, scan, screen, search, secure seize, sell, separate, shape, shift, stock, sift, simulate, solidify, solve, span, sparkle, specialize, split, steer, stimulate, strike, succeed, summarize, survey suspend, sweep, switch, synchronize, systemize, tame, teach, temporize, terminate, think, thrust, train, transfer, trap, trigger, twist, understand, unify, uphold, utilize, vary, verify, veto **and win!**

Since your mind can do all these things, it is time for you to abandon the old ways, old concepts, and old ideas, move sideways, and discover a new world — the world of new ideas. This guide is your powerful tool for generating new ideas.

So, use it . . .

HOW GOOD IS YOUR MIND?

From the previous chapters you have learned how slow and inefficient the development of human ingenuity was. Early human's ability to think innovatively was extremely poor, despite possessing the same intelligence 300,000 years ago that we do today!

The majority of new inventions, including the most critical ones, have occurred by chance or by accident. Perhaps the early humans, like today's modern descendants, found it far easier to copy what everyone else was doing; they never learned how to think for themselves. They did not know how to discover the natural laws that govern them.

It took our ancestors a very long time to learn how to feed

and clothe themselves better. How to move faster from place to place, how to fly, how to make machines to work for them, how to organize their social structures, how to make life more enjoyable or how to better communicate knowledge over large distances.

This is not to say they didn't learn many things during these periods of long and tedious intervals. I'm saying the most important skills, which they could have easily mastered if they tried, were left out almost altogether.

They did not learn how to think and teach their offspring thinking skills. If the study of history can help us understand the present better, we would heed warning to avoid those same mistakes from the past, yet for most people such study would not help at all.

It is bittersweet that, after thousands of centuries, we are only (barely) grasping the importance of this most crucial necessity: the necessity to learn and to teach others to think creatively, to innovate, to invent, to find brilliant solutions to many problems, to utilize more effectively our enormously versatile machine, the brain.

However, this unfortunate situation is your opportunity, and you have already leaped light years ahead of your fellow man. By taking steps towards developing your creative mind you are well on your way to achieving great things!

Before you embark on the Random External Stimulus Technique, it will be useful to test the state of your mind, as it is now. You should be aware of your current ability when it comes to creating new ideas and new solutions. Only then can you determine the effectiveness of this guide and REST.

You should have an opportunity, in your own privacy, to test yourself using problem examples set out for this purpose in the section on "Test Activities". It is important to recognize your limitations before you undertake the task of remedying them.

You will be your own judge. It is not likely that you will deceive yourself, although possibly. This is for your benefit and deceiving yourself would be almost as foolish as diagnosing your own illnesses.

Even a doctor must first conduct tests to reach a diagnostic conclusion before deciding what kind of medication to prescribe. If you suffer from appendicitis, a whopping cough medicine would be useless.

Regardless of your background, your occupation or your formal education, your intellect may experience difficulties, frustrations, and irritabilities when you attempt to solve the testing problem examples set out in the Test Activities section.

This is the first ability you must possess on your way to increasing your mind's creative thinking power. You can be sure that countless similar examples exist in real life, and in your own day-to-day activities.

Your mind, with its traditional, logical thinking, will habitually search for the logical answers to all your problems. When you find them, most people generally accept them as the best answers.

Unfortunately, logic fails us most of the time because we accept it so easily, if it sounds logical we do not challenge it. We now know from history that a best solution is only temporary and will be replaced by a better solution at some point.

What's needed is a new method to find better solutions not confined by logic. You will see the logical approach to these problem examples will not get you too far. This fact will be quite evident to you as soon as you start.

The examples set out in the Test Activities section are there specifically as demonstrations of the strong patterning system firmly engraved in your mind. Some problems are relatively simple while others are more complicated. You will be aware that the mind, which is not trained in creative problem-solving skills, will experience numerous difficulties when it is called upon to find ingenious solutions to various problems. You may become frustrated and annoyed when you discover how difficult it is to see the unseen, to find the hidden, to guess the unobvious.

In some cases, you will be tempted with a solution, which appears to be the correct one, only to discover later that you were wrong, that the answers are much more simplistic, more obvious than you could have ever anticipated.

The problem examples, which you are unable to solve, should be set aside until you finish reading this guide. After you do, go back to them and apply your newly acquired imaginative adaptation. You will solve them using REST and you will wonder why you did not discover the same solutions before. You will recall many occasions when you will say to yourself: Why I did not think of these answers before?

When a new idea becomes familiar and in general use, we take it for granted. It is difficult for us to place ourselves in the past when such an idea did not exist.

An ordinary zipper is an ingenious invention. We take it for granted, without realizing the zipper could have never been invented, if it was not for a brilliant thinker, its inventor. He copied the idea after observing the intricate lattice of a plant that grows in the wild, extracted this ingenious idea from nature, he applied it in business, and made a fortune.

The same is true for a myriad of other inventions, which we use casually without a second thought about their origins. You will be your own judge as to your success or failure when you attempt to solve some of these problems.

Let us test your current creativity status.

Grab a writing pad and pen or pencil. Writing for some reason engages the mind far more readily than typing or speaking.

Leave blank any areas you do not come up with a solution

for. Then later, when you understand REST come back to these exercises and see your newly found abilities.

Good Luck!

TEST YOUR MIND ACTIVITY #1– THE PENNY

In the land of IMAGINATION, when the citizens stretch their minds, their minds do not come back in their original forms and sizes.

List 20 different ideas for the use and application of a penny, 20 different things that you could do with a penny.

1._____

2._____

3._____

4._____

5._____

6._____

7. _____

8._____

9. _____

10._____

11._____

12._____

13._____

14._____

15._____

16._____

17._____

18._____

19._____

20._____

Did you come up with and write down 20 different uses or applications for a penny? If you did not, leave it for now and do it again after you learn how to use and work with REST.

TEST YOUR MIND ACTIVITY #2– "Why"

The most thought-provoking word in human language is the word "WHY."

In the land of IMAGINATION, the citizens are trained to provide an answer to every WHY, regardless how many "whys" their teachers asked.

How about you? How many whys can you pose and answer?

Try this:

Mr. Peter Unlikely is a strange person. He decided to redesign the human being from scratch. The first thing he thought was to forget the present appearance of humans. For example, he wanted his new humans to have five-foot long necks.

Start listing your whys about Mr. Unlikely's idea, and present "because" answers to each one. Every time you give a "because" answer, pose another question with another WHY. Keep going until you fill out all 12 why's.

1.WHY Mr. Peter Unlikely wanted humans to have five-foot long necks?

BECAUSE_____

2.WHY _____

BECAUSE_____

3.WHY_____

BECAUSE_____

4.WHY_____

BECAUSE_____

5.WHY_____

BECAUSE_____

6.WHY_____

BECAUSE_____

7.WHY_____

BECAUSE_____

8.WHY_____

BECAUSE_____

9.WHY_____

BECAUSE_____

10.WHY_____

BECAUSE_____

11.WHY_____

BECAUSE_____

12.WHY_____

BECAUSE_____

TEST YOUR MIND ACTIVITY #3– "TOOTHPICK"

The land of IMAGINATION is a strange country. Presume for a moment that you live there. In order to test your mind-power the rulers of Imagination have ordered you locked in a prison cell for one night. You will be shot in the morning unless . . .

Unless you come up with 50 different ideas about the use of a single toothpick.

Imagination is a country where anything goes. Grab a pen and paper and then list any idea, no matter how wild or far-fetched it might be, as long as it holds a glimmer of sense. Do this exercise FIRST as best you can, then return after understanding REST and do it again.

TEST YOUR MIND ACTIVITY #4 – "LINE"

This example is simple... or is it?

List 15 possible uses for a line?

List 15 sane or insane ideas to this question. Use every line by writing your answers down on each. "Line Use"

LINE USE: 1._____

LINE USE: 2._____

LINE USE: 3._____

LINE USE: 4._____

LINE USE: 5._____

LINE USE: 6._____

LINE USE: 7._____

LINE USE: 8._____

LINE USE: 9._____

LINE USE: 10._____

LINE USE: 11._____

LINE USE: 12._____

LINE USE: 13._____

LINE USE: 14._____

LINE USE: 15:_____

Now list 15 more ideas and answers about the same question on a separate piece of paper.

Did you think this is impossible? If you do, this guide will prove to you that there is no limit to imagination. Remember this: "In every genius there is a touch of madness."

Write your answers on each new line. If you cannot think of any more ideas, write this on each unused line: MRM (My Rigid Mind), then go back when you understand REST, and use your newfound talent. You will know how good REST is for generating new ideas, new concepts, and new thoughts.

TEST YOUR MIND ACTIVITY #5—"TWO CIRCLES"

In the land of Imagination, the students study the subject of creative thinking. Test the following examples: Draw two **identical** circles on paper. The object is to make them APPEAR as if they were different sizes.

Here are the conditions: Once you draw them you cannot touch them again in any way. They must remain intact as they are.

TEST YOUR MIND ACTIVITY #6 – "ROPE BELT"

Parents, of an eleven-year-old Imagination girl, left her all alone in the house. She had a problem. She wanted to go to bed, but the belt rope of her pyjama pants was out from the waist. Her problem was how to insert the rope belt in her pyjama pants. She could not use safety pins, wire, pencil or any other objects to thread the belt rope. Yet, she solved this problem in an ingenious way. Can you think of any way she was able solve this problem?

Write down your solution.

MY ANSWER IS:

Have you come up with anything clever? Is your imagination working the way it should? If not come back here after and try again, keep trying until you solve this problem

TEST YOUR MIND ACTIVITY #7 – "DOOR"

People of Imagination do not call the door a "door". They call it THE WAY OF ENTERING SPACES.

List 15 ways of entering spaces, 15 different ideas to use as a substitute for an ordinary door.

ENTER 1._____

ENTER 2._____

ENTER 3._____

ENTER 4._____

ENTER 5_____

ENTER 6_____

ENTER 7._____

ENTER 8._____

ENTER 9._____

ENTER 10._____

ENTER 11._____

ENTER 12._____

ENTER 13._____

ENTER 14._____

ENTER 15._____

TEST YOUR MIND ACTIVITY #8– "TWO STRINGS"

For the purpose of testing the thinking skills of their citizens and students, the educators of the Imagination posed some bizarre questions. The students had to solve a number of unusual problems, which may never come up in real life. Like any exercise, the purpose is to stretch the minds further than what is usually called upon in everyday use so that when they face real problems, using the sharpness of their imaginative minds, they could come up with brilliant solutions easily.

Later, these brilliant solutions will become even more brilliant, because in the land of Imagination, the citizens knew that there is no such a thing as the "best idea". They knew that an idea may be the best at that moment, but they also knew that a better idea was lurking somewhere, waiting to be discovered.

In this example: You stand naked in a very large room. The ceiling of the room is 12 feet high. The room is completely empty, except for two thin nylon strings hanging from the ceiling. The strings are long enough to just touch the floor. These two nylon strings are 20 feet apart. By holding one in your hand, you cannot reach the other.

Oh, yes, you share your solitude with two starved rats. Your task is to tie the two strings together.

How would you do it?

There are, in fact, two ingenious solutions to this problem, one completely different from the other. Maybe there are other solutions too.

Test yourself. How sharp is YOUR mind?

My solutions to the above problem are:

1._____

2._____

TEST YOUR MIND ACTIVITY #9- "1 + 1"

Some concepts are so well established that most people do not try to challenge them or change them. These concepts became absolute and unassailable. Nobody would tamper with them. Teachers in Imagination, however, train their people to challenge all concepts, regardless how well-established they might seem.

Their people knew that the only way to change things for the better was to be aware that behind every best idea, there are better ideas waiting to emerge. To discover the better idea, we must search for it by moving in new directions, new alternatives, even if these seem nonsensical at first. In the land of Imagination, there are "mountain size cemeteries" of old concepts and old ideas.

Here is an example. One of the most elementary concepts is: 1 + 1 equals 2. It is mathematical; it is logical, it looks correct, unchangeable, and irrefutable. Is it really? Can you challenge this concept, and come up with totally different answers? Try it, challenge it, change it. List 10 alternatives, 10 new ideas showing a possibility that one and one equals something else than two. Write down your answers,

1. 1+1 equals: _____

2 1+1 equals: _____

3. 1+1 equals: _____

4. 1+1 equals: _____

5. 1+1 equals: _____

6. 1+1 equals: _____

7. 1+1 equals: _____

8. 1+1 equals: _____

9. 1+1 equals: _____

10.1+1 equals: _____

TEST YOUR MIND ACTIVITY #10– "ZERO"

In schools of Imagination, the students had to solve many unusual problems. By forcing their minds to break out of the old traditional, straight-jacketed thinking, the Imaginations turned out geniuses at will. Here is an example:

HOW MANY NUMBERS ARE THERE IN A ZERO?

In a ZERO, there are the following numbers:

1._____

2._____

3._____

If you cannot find the answers, we will give them to you. Here they are: There are 64 numbers in a zero. These 64 numbers total 66,424,722, yes sixty-six million one hundred- twenty-four thousand-seven-hundred-twenty-two.

You may never imagine that such an answer could make any sense. Try to guess how such an answer may be possible. Use your wildest assumptions and write down your best and most imaginable guesses. If you come up with other numbers, I will classify you as half genius. How is your mental metabolism?

Okay, that completes the test. Did you get anywhere? Are you satisfied with your own cleverness? Review your answers after the reading this guide. It will be fun to compare your mind's ingenuity before and after.

A NEW WAY TO THINK

Your mind is full of powerful motors and a huge number of gears capable of shifting themselves in a vast variety of speeds. You manipulate these gears, moving them at any speed, in any direction.

It takes very little effort; it is both mental and automatic. That powerful motor is your imagination.

Albert Einstein once said: "Imagination is more important than knowledge". The validity of this statement is vividly illustrated in the case of a worker who had more imagination than knowledge.

It goes like this: The supervisor of a factory gave a rather complicated piece of machinery to a worker to put together. After a few hours, the supervisor returned with an instruction manual, which he had previously forgotten. To his great surprise, the supervisor saw that the job was completed. The machinery was all properly assembled. The supervisor asked the worker, "how did he do it"? without the instruction manual. The worker replied, "The manual would not do me any good. You see, sir, I cannot read! A long time ago, I learned that if you cannot read, you must learn how to think."

We are spending huge sums of money on education. Yet, the educational system never taught us how to THINK. The system helps us to acquire the knowledge. It moves always forward in a lineal direction, with occasional stops here and there. It has even a steering wheel capable of changing direction and moving around accidental obstacles. It functions in a logical way, systematically, sequence by sequence, from point to point, until it reaches an adequate objective.

Unlike most vehicles, this system does not include a reverse gear. It could move only forward. A well manoeuvrable vehicle must have the reverse gear, even if used only on some occasions. This lineal movement inherent in our educational system is, in fact, Logic, or Logical Thinking. It has no reverse gear.

However, the reverse gear is present in the human mind — it is Lateral Thinking, or Illogical Thinking gear. Every educator knows that young children have very creative minds. Many studies have shown the curve of their creativity rises upwards, until the time when they start to learn. Hum....

From that point on, it moves downward throughout their school life. The educational system does nothing to stimulate and expand the natural creativity of children. On the contrary, it suppresses them, discourages them, and feeds them logical thinking and knowledge only.

Of course, knowledge is important, but without imagination, knowledge is like a programmed computer; doing everything based on a predetermined set of functions and nothing outside of that.

They do not know how to change things, how to move in directions different from those, which exist in their pre-programmed electronic chips. The purpose of this guide is to change all that, to teach you how to be inventive, to apply your imagination in practice, to break away from the system of patterns implanted in your mind. In short, it teaches you how to reacquire the creative skills you naturally had as a very young child.

Consider what George Bernard Shaw once said, "I've made an international reputation for myself by thinking once or twice a week!"

A new way of thinking and REST, is what this guide is all about. So, let us go at it, step by step, leap by leap.

All thinking has two stages. Stage one is the IDEA STAGE, stage two is the PROCESSING STAGE. Before you do something, you have to start with an idea; you have to have an idea. The next step is to make that idea work.

For example, you are hungry and you want to eat. Your thoughts might follow this line of reasoning: I can go home and eat there, or I can go to McDonald's for a meal. If I go home to eat, I will save some money. On the other hand, it would be more convenient to go to McDonald's. You reach a decision. You have selected an idea out of two with which you start with. You may still have even more ideas and more alternatives.

You could have thought on the way to McDonald's, why not pick up a couple of steaks, potato salad and instead visit your sister and bring dinner?

Once you select an idea, you move from the first stage of thinking to the second stage of thinking. Now you put your idea to work. To reach McDonald's you must use your car. To do that, you face a number of motions: grabbing the keys, opening the garage door, then the car door, sitting in the driver's seat, reaching into the left pocket for the keys which are not there. Then you remember they're in your right pocket, putting your right hand in your right pocket, your fingers touch the keys and grab them. All these motions of your hands, legs and arms required thought just to get started on your initial decision of going out for something to eat.

You close the door, insert the key in the keyhole, turn it, make a series of motions to fasten the seat belts, put the car in drive, check your surroundings, and then step on the gas to go. Of course, I could drill down to an almost infinite number of details from the time you got the idea to eat at McDonald's and that moment you changed your mind to go to your sister's. Once the idea was formed, logical thinking implemented the plan.

But something happened on the way to McDonald's to change your mind; a random thought stimulated by some random external force created a new idea and you instead ended picking up some steaks and going to your sister's. It may have been just driving by a grocery store that sparked the new idea and change of plans. The point is, we constantly change our patterns of thought when a random external stimulus is applied.

While at the grocery store you buy a lottery ticket and later learn that you won the "big one". As it turned out, going to your sister's was the "best idea" of your life!

This is a simplistic example showing how the process of logical thinking works when mixed with some random external stimulus along the way. New ideas are formed.

Once the logical thinking (processing) stage takes hold, we commit ourselves to a specific action or actions. It is of utmost importance to generate many alternative ways of doing something, so that you can make the best choice possible at the time.

All undertakings in your life, whether important or not, follow this same procedure from idea to action. The principle is the same, only the details vary.

TWO STAGES OF THINKING

In our society, there is an abundance of people capable of processing ideas, once the ideas are made available.

Ample technology in all fields of human endeavour exists in our society for the second stage of thinking. Our entire educational system is geared for turning out qualified and well-trained people in the second stage of thinking. We turn out mechanized people, not idea people. We should not be surprised that we have so few idea people, so few inventors, so few innovators, so few creative thinkers.

The ratio of quality and quantity of creative thinking people, as it exists today in our society, is minimal.

However, any idea is useless, unless acted upon. An idea without action is like a car without gas. It can't move, it can look very attractive, but without energy, it is unusable. Adding gas, as the realization of a new idea backed by action, renders the car extremely useful and a vital part of our civilization.

We know that all thinking has two stages:

A. IDEA (Creative) STAGE

B. PROCESSING (Logical) STAGE

In our society we have an abundance of technology and individuals for the processing stage and a shortage for the idea stage. We have no schools, no training centers, and no means in existence to train people on how to create new ideas. This guide fills the gap by providing an exercise program to train "idea" people.

It will teach us how to generate more ideas in all of our activities. On a personal level, this guide will convert you into the skilful thinker. How do you create new ideas when you need them? A simple temporary answer is to abandon old ideas, old concepts and provoke and discover new ones.

Here, we offer you the new ways of thinking, lateral thinking, and its tool called REST (Random External Stimulus Technique).

The most important requirement in the first stage of thinking is a deliberate suspension of judgement. During the Imagination stage of creating new ideas, the purpose must be to generate a large number of alternative solutions, alternative possibilities **without evaluation, criticism, rejection, and premature judgement or choice**.

In the idea stage, you merely exercise the quality of our imagination. You look at a situation or a specific problem from every conceivable angle.

Brainstorm ideas by rapidly writing down everything that comes to mind.

Some ideas will appear impossible, strange, or even silly, but write them down anyways. Later you will evaluate them. For now, DO NOT interrupt the creative process by stopping to "think" about each idea logically. **Later when you exit your creative state** you can then consider all the ideas you generated with your logical mind.

Sometimes, an impossible idea could trigger a new idea that leads to a real solution, which you never considered. In mining and processing gold, it takes four tons of ore to produce one ounce of gold! So, it is with creativity, but once you find the vein your creativity will flow.

Consider, for example, the statement: "Money runs on wheels". There may not be a reason for making such a statement, but now you have it. Can you do anything with it? As you know, money does not run on wheels. This statement makes no sense, because it is illogical. Do you think that there is nothing you can do with this statement?

Would you discard it as worthless,
nonsensical, silly?

Now, let us suspend judgement and apply the principle of REST to the same statement, and see where it may lead us.

Can money really run?

Why not?

A marathon runner may carry some money while running.
A cyclist runs on wheels using muscle power to move it.

Some people have invested in the production of bicycles. A car runs on wheels, and it costs a great deal of money, it has a dollar value; therefore, a car is money that moves on wheels. A car also often transports money; therefore, money runs on wheels all the time. The presses that print money have many wheels, cogs, and rollers, therefore the above statement may trigger new ideas about ways of manufacturing, transporting or designing something.

One could go on and on listing many thoughts, many associations, and many ideas about this supposedly worthless statement, which at first glance, seems sheer nonsense.

If you judge the validity of that statement too prematurely, apply criticism to it and reason logically about it, you will reject it outright as completely valueless. Your logical judgement will destroy any possibility of creative thinking to find some useful ideas from it.

In the first stage of thinking, the idea stage, we want to generate a large number of possibilities with no thought given to merit. At this stage our imagination is fully engaged and we are brainstorming, writing down everything that pops into our mind without delay.

This process is extremely invigorating; our brain starts producing dopamine, a chemical released by nerve cells to send signals to other nerve cells which functions as a neurotransmitter. Your mind is awakened to a much higher plane as thoughts flood the mind with ideas. One experience of being totally in the "zone" is enough to ignite the flame of your imagination.

At first this process will feel strange, maybe even stupid. This is your habit of being logical, resisting the change. In this stage of thinking, you should not make any decisions, which may commit you to undertake a definite action.

You do not commit yourself to an irreversible action; you are simply GATHERING IDEAS AND ALTERNATIVES. Later, when you have accumulated a great many ideas, you examine them, using rational and logical reasoning. Then you will know which idea, among the large number you created is the most promising, the most acceptable and practical. When you have a large number of ideas to choose from, your mind should have no difficulties in selecting the best one available at the time.

Subsequently, you can embark on a number of steps necessary to realize the best choice. Enter into the creative zone again using REST to further explore the ideas you created on the first round. At some point, you enter the second stage of thinking — the processing stage.

The human mind uses two basic types of thinking:

1. LOGICAL THINKING

2. NON-LOGICAL THINKING or IMAGINATION

Let us examine both types of thinking and find out how they work. This is important because the basis of this guide is the understanding of these two thinking processes.

LOGICAL THINKING

This type of thinking is the most commonly used way the human mind functions. The fundamental operation of logical thinking is to follow a pattern determined by a set of known rules. We judge if an idea is right or wrong based on known principles. If an Idea fits within our firmly established ways of looking at things then it is easily accepted as a good idea. If the idea does not fit, we reject it without further analysis.

The word "no" is simply a very effective way of stopping any further train of thought. Once we use such a method to cut a train of thought, we commit ourselves to a final judgement without exploring further. This judgement reduces the possibilities down to either accepting or rejecting an idea.

Even if such an idea retains some useful elements, saying "no" stops the flow of creativity dead in its tracks. Such an idea may have later proved to be of great value.

Further consideration is simply cut off, and irrevocably terminated. What does the logical thinking do? It is the judge, jury and executioner. Logical thinking judges whether an idea fits in with the established patterns of experience or established concepts, then condemns everything that does not fit. For example, if I were to suggest that 1 + 1 = 1, you would reject that idea, because you know from previous experience you were taught in our numerical system this is not true. If I were to suggest that it is a good idea to eat soup with a knife, you would reject this idea, because you could not see how that would work. From your previous experience, you know that you could not eat soup with a knife.

If I were to suggest that Albert Einstein was the emperor of France, you would object immediately, because this idea does not fit the historical record you were taught.

The principal function of the human brain is to follow, faithfully, the patterns of experience. An elaborate system of patterns is well established in the mind of every individual. Our lives run totally on patterns.

We learn from experience that certain words mean certain things when used in certain context, without which language would be nearly impossible to understand. We learn to coordinate the movements of our legs, otherwise walking would be impossible. When you see the picture of a house, the image in your mind will be that of a house, not of an elephant, because (from your previous experience) you recognize the house.

This patterning system is well ingrained in your mind. If someone would suggest something different or contrary, you would judge it to be wrong and reject it outright. Logical thinking is like a mathematical formula. Every step of the way must be correct, so that you can be certain the result will also be correct.

Logical thinking is a YES/NO binary

system that works like a computer.

We rationalize through YES or NO decisions by referencing the total sum of all our experience to accept or reject an idea, we make a choice, we decide, we commit ourselves one way or another. Logical thinking is immensely effective in implementing ideas once they are available, therefore, logical thinking is a necessary second stage of thinking.

As much as the logical thinking is good at processing ideas, it is unable to generate new ideas.

All new ideas seem to run contrary to the established ones; otherwise, they would not be regarded as new. Almost every scientific theory and revolutionary invention has, at first, been attacked as unsound or preposterous because it did not fit the generally accepted and established thinking patterns.

The automobile, when first introduced, was rejected by most people as never being able to replace the horse and buggy.

Galileo was placed under house arrest for years because he claimed the earth was not at the center of the universe and that the earth circled around the sun.

When in 1938, Chester Carlson invented Xerography, some of the largest North American Corporations rejected his invention.

His idea of using static electricity for copying on ordinary paper was contrary to scientific knowledge of that time and all scientists rejected it, declaring it was impossible.

When, in 1857 Louis Pasteur, discovered the existence of germs and viruses, all scientists of that period ridiculed him. His ideas were so far from the accepted thought patterns of the day his contemporaries labelled him as a quack.

When, in 1892 Rudolf Diesel, invented the diesel engine, he could not find financiers to invest into the production of his concept. Nobody believed that such an engine could be commercially successful. His idea was new, therefore, unacceptable to the society in which he lived. We know now that without his engine, most of our present technological advances would not have been possible.

Yet, he died a poor man. In 1913, he sailed from Antwerp to England, in a last attempt to persuade the British Admiralty about the validity of his new engine for large military ships. Destiny was unkind to him. When crossing the English Channel, he fell overboard and drowned.

Many revolutionary ideas have been rejected as being only fantasies of those individuals who have their heads in the clouds. Alone are the inventors who dare to dream beyond accepted norms!

In some cases where major changes to the world occurred, the inventions responsible were recognized for their significance only after their creators had passed.

Since logical thinking processes ideas, let us see what kind of thinking is necessary to create them. To create new ideas and provoke the mind to jump out of the established patterns of thought, we need to invoke our imagination.

TWO TYPES OF IMAGINATION

Two types of imagination are used to develop new ideas: synthetic and creative. Having an imagination is the source of new ideas and REST using lateral thinking is the method by which you stimulate your imagination.

Lateral thinking, as formulated by the world-famous psychologist Dr. Edward de Bono, is very different from logical thinking, because it is based on movement rather than judgement.

Lateral thinking is a DELIBERATE departure from logical — sequential thinking. Lateral Thinking is NEVER concerned with whether an idea is right or wrong. An idea is only a stepping-stone to another new and original idea.

An idea, which seems wrong, may lead somewhere very useful. An idea, which is actually wrong, may lead to a correct solution. An idea, which seems contradictory and wide off the mark, may still contain something useful. Lateral thinking is concerned ONLY with exploration, not with proof.

Lateral Thinking moves for the sake of moving. It creates new directions instead of following one.

LATERAL THINKING GENERATES NEW PATHWAYS and ORIGINAL IDEAS.

We know that great many discoveries and inventions have happened by chance and accident. In previous pages we clearly demonstrated how bad and inadequate the human mind is when it is called upon to come up with new ideas, new and better ways to look at things.

Humans have not undertaken a serious effort to provoke the production of new ideas by a systematic method that could be taught in our schools and colleges. Only a small number of creative people use thought provoking devices. Only the most creative minds in our world talk about provocative thoughts for opening up new alleyways to new Ideas.

Poets use provocative process when creating beautiful and unusual verses. Painters and sculptors are forever breaking away from the established patterns to provoke new insights. Some creative individuals have used bizarre ways in an attempt to put themselves in a creative mood and incite new ideas.

Here are some known examples: Schiller kept rotten apples in his desk! Shelley and Rousseau remained bareheaded in the sunshine. Bossier worked in a cold room with his head wrapped in furs.

Milton, Descartes, Leibniz, and Rossini stretched out. Carlyle worked in a noise proof room. Balzac wore a monkish garb. Goethe and Schiller immersed their feet in ice-cold water. D'Annunzio, Forney and Frost worked only at night.

The importance of chance inputs is now readily acknowledged in science and art. It may have been a chance observation, a mistake in an experiment, a chance meeting of two people. Chance input from the outside, when it happens, causes a breakout from conventional and established patterns of thought. The input has to be a chance because to find the solution we seek, we usually explore among current well-established ideas we already have.

New ideas cannot suddenly jump out of the usual, predictable, and familiar ideas and concepts. A new idea is new, because it is strange, unfamiliar, and it does not fit existing molds.

The main characteristics of Lateral Thinking and its basic processes are:

A. IMPOSSIBLE IDEAS AS STEPPING-STONES.

B. DELIBERATE USE OF RANDOM OR CHANCE EXTERNAL STIMULUS.

C. CHALLENGING PRESENTLY ACCEPTED IDEAS.

IMPOSSIBLE IS WHERE LOGICAL THINKING ENDS AND CREATIVE THINKING BEGINS

Lateral thinking creates thoughts which seem ridiculous or foolish that are used for the stimulation of new thinking as a temporary step towards an original and possible "good" idea. It is very easy for a human mind to switch from an impossible idea to a possible one. The mind possesses an elasticity, which allows it to connect things that are seemingly unconnectable. Suspending judgement, criticism, and rejection are the basis for creative thinking. Let us see how some "impossible" ideas could provoke the mind to find new and unexpected avenues, leading towards ingenious discoveries.

Here is an impossible idea:

"Lottery is an excellent meal, when broiled on a toboggan"

Using logical thinking process, we will reject this idea immediately, and consider it absurd. It makes no sense at all. How can a lottery be an excellent meal? How can we broil anything on a toboggan?

This is sheer nonsense.

However, using the Lateral thinking process, we activate areas of our mind seldom used, allowing any and all ideas to stand, just to see if they can lead us somewhere.

Our lateral thinking mind may take these routes:

Lottery might become a meal. We will imagine for a moment that the lottery is a meal indeed.

> 1- A charitable organization could run a lottery and use its proceeds to buy food for needy families.
>
> 2- We could start a new business by offering the public tickets to win meals for two at the top ten restaurants in the area using the lottery method. We could offer thousands of such tickets at say one tenth of their real value. The winners would enjoy eating at the chef's table in the most exclusive restaurants, free of charge.
>
> 3- In the early Lotteries they usually involved a drum to told hold and mix the tickets. The drum is spun and then a ticket is drawn. A special drum could be used for preparing a meal. By first mixing various food ingredients, the drum could then cook meals in it. Something like a rotisserie, but instead of rotating a spit, rotate the drum. The drum could become a new cooking invention!

Can we broil a meal on a toboggan?

> 1- Children use a toboggan to slide on the snow. Frozen meals for children could be made and packaged in a special container resembling a toboggan, just pop it in the oven and voila', call them fun meals!.

Here is another impossible idea:

"COMB HAIR WITH A BALL"

Here, again, we have a completely nonsensical idea. Before we discard this idea as silly and worthless, let us see if we could extract any value from it, and use it as a stepping-stone leading us to a new and useful idea.

We use a ball to play games. Balls come in many different sizes, colours and textures. With a ball we can throw, bounce, bat, catch, and roll.

1- Maybe we can develop a ball with comb like teeth that clamps onto hair and becomes a new fashion accessory.

2- Maybe we can create a flat round shaped comb to hold a ponytail rather than using an elastic band, another fashion accessory.

3- Could we make a round shaped dispenser that combs and dispenses a hair colour?

4- Can we make a comb with a ball point pen like tip to apply scalp medication that will not get on the hair?

5- Why not a vacuum cleaner attachment for hair? A hair dryer equipped with round-like prongs. (Oh Ya, that has been done, I think it's called a diffuser)

6- A helmet equipped with comb-like nozzles as scalp massager or scalp scanner.

We could go on and on listing all kinds of ideas, unusual ideas, triggered by the above nonsensical statement.

Some ideas may be "far-out", some may be even undesirable, but some contain the kernel of a new and marketable invention. The main point here is to show you how an impossible idea could move your mind from a static position to many new directions.

Your mind can not do this on its own.

REST opens up the Lateral thinking process that takes your mind in new directions; otherwise, you are stuck going around in circles following the old well traveled paths of your mind.

Lateral thinking helps us to move for the sake of moving. Where it leads is of no concern. Our minds know how to transform that movement into new thinking, new mental triggers and ultimately the discovery of new and original usable ideas.

By discarding an idea as worthless, you reach a dead end, stop the creative process and halt any creative movement from that point. The only thing left to do then is to start from the beginning and try another road, an established road, a recognizable road or another logical road which ultimately takes you down well traveled paths.

This is fine for those who are not interested in new ideas, but not so good for the creative individuals.

Lateral thinking does not have an end. It is open ended. The end could and often does become the next beginning, the middle, another dimension, another stepping-stone.

Lateral thinking utilizes the natural flexibility of the mind. It stretches the mind in many directions, without the danger of breaking it. It helps the mind to form a habit of exercising imagination.

Right and wrong, YES or NO, do not exist in the Lateral thinking process. Lateral thinking is fluid thinking. It surges uphill, downhill, sideways, up, down, and in every other conceivable direction. It is limitless like the imagination. It moves, and moves, and moves . . .

USE OF THE RANDOM EXTERNAL STIMULUS TECHNIQUE

This entire guide was designed to demonstrate your mind is an inexhaustible source of ideas, if you train and develop your creative thinking skills. We know that chance inputs, and chance happenings were, in the past, the main movers in advancing our civilization.

REST is a method specifically created to turn out chance inputs at will. We use this method extensively throughout this guide. You do not have to wait for the chance inputs to happen by accident.

With the technique described in this guide YOU CREATE HAPPY ACCIDENTS AT WILL.

CHALLENGE ESTABLISHED CONCEPTS

Old concepts and old ideas are powerful barriers that stop the flow of new concepts and new ideas. Every time a new revolutionary idea emerges out of the mind of a creative individual, it is at first rejected as being silly, or even harmful.

The history of every notable invention is full of vicious attacks on innovation and creators of such invention. When in 1543 Nicolas Copernicus came up with the theory of movements of celestial bodies in the universe, showing that the Sun, not the Earth, as the central body around which all heavenly bodies move, Protestant leaders attacked him and accused him of being a heretic. They alleged his new theory was contrary to Scriptures. Even 90 years later, in 1632, when Galileo Galilei discovered four of Jupiter's satellites, and provided clear proof to those that not all heavenly bodies revolve around the earth, the Holy Office in Rome tried him as a heretic. They banned his treatise as being sacrilegious because it supported the theory that the sun is the immovable center of the universe.

There are still people today who claim the earth is flat.

When Henry Ford started mass production of cars, most people said: "The automobile will never replace the horse and buggy." They considered the automobile as being a toy, a gadget, a novelty without any practical value.

Most people regard existing concepts as the absolute truths with which nobody should tamper with.

Even when some well-established concepts were demolished and replaced with new ones, many people refused to accept their validity. When a new idea replaces an old one, it simply means that the new idea is much superior and overwhelmingly better than the old one.

Once established, people adapted, used, and then embraced the new idea.

The younger generations easily accept new ideas. Ideas and concepts change and the pace at which they change is accelerating. Everything around us never stays the same long. Change comes because there is no such thing as the best idea. There is only the best idea, at the moment.

The history of our civilization is the history of ideas. More than that, it is the history of change, the evolution of change.

The pace of change, however, has been painfully slow in the ancient past. Fortunately, beginning with the Industrial Revolution, which started in mid-nineteenth century, that pace accelerated ever faster. Just a couple of hundred years ago, humans could have lived their entire life without experiencing a single revolutionary change.

A few hundred years ago, mankind lived through centuries without any major changes in their lives, ignoring the technical knowledge they possessed. Going back tens of thousands of years, we know that it took hundreds, sometimes thousands of centuries to effect a major change.

Today we live in a different world. The pace of change has advanced to such an extent that every ten years, or every five years, some major break through happens. Many people experience psychological discomfort because they are unable to accept the fast pace of changes, and adopt them.

The memory chip in a computer is doubling in capacity every two years. This means that it halves in physical size with the same capacity every two years! Cell size robots are already being developed that can be injected into the blood stream with a syringe that seek out and destroy only cancer cells!

Our museums are full of relics from the past, from various historical eras that, at their time, were revolutionary, world changing inventions. There is a museum, the Smithsonian Institution in Washington, where one can see the relic of the first computer called UNIVAC, that was used commercially. It takes up an entire room; some of today's children's toys have more computing power!

We are creating new machines, in ever increasing numbers, capable of doing much of the human work. There are many plants presently in operation, which are completely automated, where manual labour is non-existent. The factory operates in complete darkness because no one is in there. A few workers supervise the machines through a control room and only when maintenance is required or a breakdown occurs, are the lights turned on.

This process continues as smarter machines replace more and more manual labourers.

The path to the future is well defined. Our lives will become easier as machines do more and more of our chores. It will be up to each individual to decide what they want to do with their lives.

As lifestyle changes, we must change as well. The change we are experiencing now simply means this: the more you embrace creativity, the happier and more fulfilled you will be.

To assure you succeed, you must **train** your mind to THINK, and be capable of producing new ideas when you need them. **New ideas are only possible if you challenge and change existing concepts starting with your own.**

Let us see what happens when we challenge some firmly established concepts.

Here are two examples:

A. A CAR MUST HAVE FOUR ROUND WHEELS

B. EDUCATION EXPANDS THE MINDS OF PEOPLE

If we do not challenge an old idea, it remains old and unchanged. Unless we make a deliberate effort to challenge it with a new and better idea, it will remain the same.

In the first stage of thinking, we use our imagination, in an effort to search and discover new ideas. First, we must mentally "let go" of established concepts to clear the path for exploration. Then, if we do not succeed in the process, if we do not discover a better idea, we have not caused any harm.

So, let us proceed.

A CAR MUST HAVE FOUR WHEELS. To challenge this statement let us assume the following reasoning: Suppose a car would have three wheels. The cost of one entire wheel, tire, and axle could be eliminated. It may be more manoeuvrable.

What if a car would run on two wheels? This thought might trigger the idea to design a car with two wide rollers instead of four wheels. What would happen if the car could run on one wheel? Maybe some kind of new wheel designed like a ball would be possible. Perhaps a one roller-type wheel or a continuous belt type system could be possible. What would happen if a car would have no wheels at all? Could it function? A boat is, in effect, the car without wheels.

Can the boat become a car? Can a car fly?

Certainly, both already exist.

We could design a car, similar to a hovercraft, so that it rides on a cushion of air. This car could traverse all kinds of terrain.

What about the round wheels? Suppose we equip a car with a set of square wheels.

What would happen?

The ride would be very bumpy.
But can a bumpy ride be useful?

Perhaps we might make the streets in our large cities conveyer belts that will lock onto square wheels.

We can make city roads bumpy and uncomfortable to ride on; this might discourage motorists from using them, leave their cars at home, and take transit.

We could eliminate the traffic congestion.

We could construct a square-wheeled vehicle to serve as a continuous mixer, maybe for concrete? A bumpy ride would produce constant up and down motion, which could mix concrete on the way to the job site.

We could attach a trailer-like container with square wheels to a truck and use it as an amusement ride. Could a bumpy ride be desirable for people? We could put people in such vehicles, make the vehicle look like a T-Rex and simulate riding a live T-Rex. Amusement parks would gobble this up. Perhaps such a vehicle could promote a new sport, T-Rex Polo!:-)

EDUCATION ENLIGHTENS THE MINDS OF PEOPLE.

This statement is logical and would be considered a fact by most people. However, we now know to contest old established norms. Let's try to come up with different ideas about education.

Let us challenge its validity. Education, as it is familiar to us, is a schooling system; in fact, it is several schooling systems: Kindergarten, Elementary, Secondary, College, University, Post Graduation, Specialized Studies, Doctorates.

If the statement we are challenging is true, then the most educated individuals should have the best minds. The truth is that this is not so. The most educated people may be good in the fields of their specializations, but they are notoriously poor thinkers!

Their minds consider only the cold, inflexible Aristotelian logic they were taught by the education system described. We know that people, who have strong logical minds, cannot generate new and revolutionary ideas.

Edison, who possessed the most inventive mind of all times, had no schooling. His mother taught him how to write, read, and some elementary mathematics. However, he has to his credit well over a thousand useful inventions!

Had he gone through the educational system in a normal and orderly way, he would be sure, based on the engineering knowledge, that the continuous burning of a filament in a vacuum would not be possible.

He would have not tested some 6,000 different materials to find the best filament, and perhaps we would have had to wait a 100 more years for the invention of the incandescent bulb.

Albert Einstein was a poor student in school. If he had accepted the scientific theories of his time, mainly Newton's theories in physics, considered unshakable truths, he would have not challenged that knowledge and we would still be waiting for someone to discover the theory of relativity and the nature of atomic and sub-atomic particles.

Churchill, probably the greatest political leader of our era, was not particularly successful in school. His mind was too restless to accept the conformity of well-established ideas. His success, his accomplishments were due to his creative mind. He was unafraid to challenge the established ideas and create new ones, when he needed them.

Challenging this concept about education, might induce us to create new teaching methods, based on new knowledge about the human mind and its power. We may examine, in more details, the ways and the means employed by famous inventors, artists, sculptors, military geniuses, political geniuses, literary geniuses, to learn what made them what they were.

We might learn their methods, their ingenuity about innovation and inventiveness. We might create a new educational system capable of turning the ordinary people into geniuses.

Grab a pen and paper and challenge the following concepts. Come up with new ideas resulting from your challenge. Do this activity first WITHOUT the use of REST, later with REST Compare the differences.

1. ONLY HUMANS CAN TALK, Challenge:

2. BEST MATERIAL FOR PRINTING BOOKS IS PAPER. Challenge:

3. A HOUSE MUST HAVE SOLID FOUNDATIONS. Challenge:

4. WITHOUT LIGHT, WE CANNOT SEE. Challenge:

5. WOOL IS LIGHTER THAN STEEL. Challenge:

ASSOCIATION OF IDEAS- SYNTHETIC IMAGINATION

Your mind's synthetic imagination functions by associating one idea with another. This process generates a continuous combination of known ideas in a new way creating an endless chain that ties all the thoughts together.

One of the most powerful functions of the mind is its ability to associate ideas. Plato and Aristotle, the Greek philosophers, who lived 2,300 years ago, formulated the laws of association of ideas, sometimes known as Free Associations.

It was Aristotle (384 - 322 B.C.) who discovered and formulated the three laws of association of Ideas. They are:

1. CONTIGUITY

2. SIMILARITY

3. CONTRAST

Many other principles of association emerged through the years, but these laws as formulated by Aristotle remain basic. I offer you a brief explanation of each law of association:

CONTIGUITY: This law explains how associations work by the stimulation of contact or nearness. A saddle may remind you of a horse, tree of a forest, foot of a shoe, glove of a hand, and so on.

SIMILARITY: This law explains how the similar things produce a chain of thoughts. A cat could remind you of a tiger, a tent may provoke the mental connection with a log cabin, the human eye is similar to a photographic camera, a staircase is similar to an escalator, etc.

CONTRAST: This law explains how we associate things,

which contrast one another. A midget may trigger an association of a giant, day reminds you of night, a sad face is a contrast to a happy face, black and white are contrasting colors, tall and short, big and small, heaven and hell, God and devil, etc.

It is not important to make any special distinction between these laws of associations. The phenomenon of associations is, in effect, an automatic process, and your mind knows how to use it any time. The different laws of association prove that such laws do exist.

In this guide, we shall treat the associations of ideas as a natural faculty of the mind, irrespective of the differences of their laws. It does not matter by which law of associations your thoughts flow, as long as they flow and result in an abundant movement.

We explained them briefly to make you aware that such laws do exist. We use the associations of ideas as an automatic and practical way to put ideas in flowing sequences.

The phenomenon of free associations stirs our imagination with our memory and causes a flow of thoughts to follow one another.

The power of free associations is a cardinal principle of psychology.

Associations work harder for those whose imagination is more intense and whose minds function better. They move through their memory vividly. The more a thought lends itself to the associative process, the more it is capable of coming up with new and original ideas. Production of ideas depends upon the contents of your mind, and how you mix the experiences that are in it.

Imagination serves as a catalyst in this process.

Associations work through partial identification, too. The mind creates a connection of various seemingly unrelated parts, probing deeper and deeper, reaching for particular elements that are parts of our own life experiences. Dreams are sometimes created this way.

Associations are uniquely and exclusively ours. They are the reflections of the individual's cumulative memory.

The road to associations of ideas moves the mind toward directions determined by our personal experiences, and the retention of these experiences in our memory.

The sight of a new model car may trigger associations of the first car you owned. You may recall the events surrounding that first purchase. Perhaps your mate or your friend was there. You may remember the salesperson, the showroom, the praise or criticism of your peers, and so on, and on. The mind produces the free associations through variety of sensory perceptions. It receives them by our five senses.

The mind absorbs huge number of inputs and stores them into its memory bank via our senses.

The events, good or bad, will trigger direct associations. The chain of connecting thoughts may lead you to the distant past, the present, and the future.

For example, you walk near a restaurant, and your nostrils detect a familiar odour. By a chain of associations, you may recall your mother's cooking. You will remember meals that she prepared for you. You may remember your mother, details of your relationship, events from your childhood, and much more.

Taste, pleasant or unpleasant, could similarly trigger new associations, and link up the events, which were parts of your experience.

Sweetness of a candy may remind you of your sister who grabbed the last candy from your mother's jar. The sweetness of a certain candy may remind you of a party where you met the love of your life. A bitter taste may remind you of some difficult and unpleasant period in your past.

Any input by your five senses, could trigger a powerful chain of associations. When you hear a certain tune, you may think of the first dance with your mate, the location, the music, and the time when this event took place.

Similarly, the sound of a voice may remind you of someone else, perhaps a radio announcer or a friend whose voice has the same or similar character. Touch also can evoke many associations. For example, touching the skin of a peach may produce memories of your first kiss. You continue with these associations and remember many details of your relationship.

Touching a hot surface may provoke thoughts about bad burns you may have experienced in the past. Your memory stores all perceptions in a memory bank and receives them through your five senses.

Just reading these paragraphs likely triggered long forgotten thoughts from your past.

The mind never stops thinking. Try it. Decide to think of nothing. You will realize that it is impossible.

Or is it? Try it now before reading further...

How long before your inner voice started chattering about something? Almost instantly, I bet.

Now try this: close your eyes, take a deep breath and ask yourself, "I wonder what my next thought will be"?

You should have experienced a longer moment of "total" mind control, a state of mind where absolute clarity is reached.

Practising Meditation develops mastery of clarity of thought. It is the Mount Everest of developing mind power, not a topic that can be given proper instruction here. But is available at www.CompetentMinds.com.

An entire chain of associations can start with a single word or object. The chain of thoughts, triggered by a specific word or object, could have a powerful effect on you.

Just as the small force of a finger squeezing the trigger of a gun sets off a chain of events starting with a massive explosion. The following events that result from such a small force can be devastating.

The person, who released the first atomic bomb from an airplane used a very small force to activate its triggering mechanism, but the power of the bomb exploding was so enormous that it obliterated an entire city.

A word could generate a similar effect upon your mind, and cause the release of enormous power, which may become useful, constructive, and everlasting.

Since the stored memory of each person is different, the resulting associations will also be different. There are no two people on earth whose stored memory is identical.

Let us try some associations and see how they work when triggered by a single word. Of course, your associations may be completely different because your mind is different and your stored memory is different. This difference is essential, otherwise we would all think alike.

This dynamic difference makes us different from one another.

FREE ASSOCIATIONS BY A WORD

1. SANDPAPER: Abrasion, polishing, roughness, woodwork, wood dust, sand, beach sandcastle, ocean swim, bikini.

2. BONUS: Special reward, work over and above call of duty, extra money, vacation, buying of gifts, additional efforts, exploitation, incentives for workers, political fraud.

3. GERM: Sickness, contamination, microscopic observations, infection, doctors, hospitals, epidemic, research, Pasteur, seed, growth, penicillin, cold, running nose, pills, hot tea.

3. SIEVE: Separation, fine granular matter, passing through, selection, fine mesh, grading, flour, baking, pastries, sugar.

4. PROPOSAL: Love, marriage, man, women, proposition, family, intentions, honour, bind, connection, ring, gentle bribe, seduction, written document, business plans.

6. DYNAMITE: Explosive, blasting, mine and mining, ore, Nobel, fuse, unstable personality, power, uncontrollable strength, sticks, robbery, blowing a safe, destruction, anarchy.

7. EXPLORATION: Search, unknown territory, find, curiosity, surprise, historic explorers, captor, oppressors, colonization, abuse, Indian wars, dislocation, unfairness.

8. DICE: Game of chance, something for nothing, gambling, unruliness, handling money, dots, six sided objects, dice table, shouting, dice throw, diced meat, cubes, ice, forming.

9. ALLELUIA: Religions, praying and prayer, choir, Christianity, religious prosecutions, repetitive chant, echo, voices, bible, Apostles, indoctrination, propaganda, appeal.

10. HURRICANE: Force of wind, destruction, floods, demolition of homes and properties, homeless people, human misery, power of nature, punishment, invisible force, dust clouds, air contamination.

Every association in our examples follows one or more laws of association. It is not important by which law or by what route one produces associations, as long as the flow of ideas keeps moving. You may start with the first word and link it up with the next one, which might have a similar meaning with the first one, and end up with new associations that may not have any similarity with the first one.

The point to remember is that it is not important in which direction your mind moves, as long as it moves. When the mind is in motion, it will not stop; the motion accelerates instead of subsiding. You could go on and on to infinity. The process of free associations is an endless one.

It is very important that you develop the habit of using associations, because the associative process is the fundamental element of creative thinking and REST.

You should carry on association exercises with attention

and diligence. They are fun to do and they are the most effective methods for the fruitful use of this guide and REST.

FREE ASSOCIATION EXERCISES

Grab a pen and paper and write down *your* associations using bellow-listed words as starters. Fill every line regardless if you have difficulty in coming up with "clever" associations.

HARNESS

SAUCE

LATCH

MASQUERADE

LEARNER

RENT

DRIFTWOOD

SLIDE

ADULTERY

GROIN

SIDEBURNS

RACE

SAUNA

CHICKEN

HOLLOWNESS

RANDOM WORDS AND THE REST

The English language contains more than 16,000 different nouns and verbs. They represent a powerful source for REST. Pictures are also a great source for REST, but for the purpose of this guide we will use random words. Words pump new blood into the entire methodology of thinking and stimulate the discontinuity of patterns in the mind of the user.

REST enables the mind to free itself from overpowering logical thinking and produces unexpected inputs necessary for the first stage of thinking. Random Words bombard your imagination, thus helping you to create new ideas, new insights. Random words, individually or in groups of two or three, produce unsought, chance, random external stimuli which otherwise would not be possible.

Random words serve as a deliberate ignition of creative thought and move the mind in many different directions. They provoke a movement or sake of movement; the mind decides where this movement will lead it.

The main impact of random words on the mind is their ability to produce the interruption of set patterns, which crowd the mind of all individuals.

The following points characterize this method of discontinuity:

1. The stimulus comes from outside, (external).

2. We do not choose the stimuli, (random) therefore, they are truly unrelated.

3. By injecting the "Random External Stimulus" into a problem situation, we introduce a "pattern interrupt" almost immediately.

4. The stimulus links up with a problem situation and establishes a new starting point, a new pathway. (Lateral thinking)

5 The stimulus becomes relevant AFTER it has been introduced, and its effect creates a newer thought in a situation or a problem. (Logical Thinking)

6. Using natural flexibility of the mind, the stimulus triggered by a random word turns the irrelevancy into relevancy. It makes sense out of nonsense.

The fundamental benefit of random word stimulation is that the initial effect is not relevant. The relevance becomes real only AFTER the effect stimulated by a random word. By its design, REST achieves an absolute randomness. There is no way of knowing which word, or group of words, will be used next.

This is how total randomness functions. It creates the total chance inputs for a powerful effect upon the mind of the user. You should not select or choose the words which you might like or dislike.

You should use ANY WORD or words regardless if you like them or not.

Grab a dictionary and open it to any page and without looking place you finger on the page. Use that word as your random external stimulus.

You can request Think Tank SFI (software for innovation) at www.LateralThinkingCourse.com if you wish to accelerate your results with REST

It is important to assure the complete random impact. You do not choose the words; you take them as they come.

This is of UTMOST IMPORTANCE, because the chance inputs and the randomness must be your primary objective. You can use words that are adjectives, adverbs, or nouns. However, nouns are best because, after a considerable study and experimentation, I have concluded that the nouns facilitate the production of associations significantly better than adverbs or adjectives.

The first word or words you randomly pick may be considered unpromising, at first.

Do not trust your first impression; it is your logical mind controlling you. Stay with your selection, and make an honest effort to extract FUNCTION, DIRECT MEANING, ASSOCIATION and HUMOR from it, before you continue to get new selection. It is useless to move on until you come across a word, which you like better or find more promising.

That is self defeating.

You would destroy the effect of randomness. This is a very important point I can not stress enough because as soon as any intention for preference creeps in, you lose the whole effect of random words.

Moreover, you substantially reduce your effort to use the random words as we explain here. You would be inclined to pass over one word and pick up an "easier" one. For this reason, it is best to extract ideas, associations, and mental connections from EVERY WORD before you jump on the next one.

You will find that quite often the best ideas come from a word that does not look promising at first glance.

In the beginning, it may be somewhat difficult, but as you gradually develop confidence and skill in REST, it will become easier and feel more natural.

Once you have a random word, you should use it in a practice problem. Besides the problems presented in this course, Lateral thinking puzzles offer great practice. ThinkTank SFI comes with a library of Lateral Thinking Puzzles to practice with. The answers to these puzzles are provided but I strongly urge you not to look at the answers until you have come up with your own answer. Once you have something that makes sense, only then should you look at the answer provided for comparison only. Remember there is no "best" idea, there is always a better solution lurking around and your goal is to find it. Have fun and laugh; it's only practice! You should try to force an association produced by a random word on a problem and see how relevant the two can become. You will notice that after a while, some sort of a link-up develops between the two.

The link-up may be direct or indirect. One random word (the catalyst) leads you to another and another by a series of chain links, it directs you toward new ideas. To generate the link-up, you must pay attention to the original random word and develop it in all possible directions.

At each point, you should refer back to the problem at hand to see what relevance each new development could have.

For instance, the problem might be of motivating factory workers for better performance and higher efficiency. Let us assume random word you have been given is "FOX."

Our thought speculation might work the following ways:

FOX — an animal that kills chickens: the idea, reward good producers by giving them periodically a gift of a chicken or a turkey.

FOX — a furry animal — fur indicates comfort: provide more comfort in the factory, paint machinery in attractive colors, install more pleasant lighting, music, more comfortable work benches and seats.

FOX — an animal characterized by cleverness. Run a contest among the workers for ways to improve their conditions and give awards to the best ideas.

FOX — fox fur which women and men wear around their necks. This may suggest the idea of providing suitable gifts to the best performers. Motivate a male worker by rewarding him and his wife with a dinner at a high-end restaurant.

In using random words, you could stick to a particular line of development, but it is better to accumulate as many suggestions as possible at first. Later, you will decide which idea would be the most practical, reasonable, and effective.

Your path would be from idea to implementation!

How much time should you spend searching for the most promising ideas? As long as it takes, but there is a danger of boredom and frustration if you spend too long a time.

On a personal note, one of the questions in this very guide took me weeks to solve. When I did solve it, I slapped myself on the forehead and said "Doh" like Homer Simpson. And the answer came at the strangest of times. I was walking my dog when the solution just "appeared to me". The answer was so obvious that I was stunned that I had not come up with the solution immediately when I first read the problem.

As your experience and your skills grow, you will make full use of a random word in a relatively short time. Use enough of your time to sufficiently relate a random word and make it relevant. However, the more effort you put in developing a large number of relevancies, the more rewarding your results will be.

With every consecutive try, more and better ideas will emerge. This is why we recommend going as far as you can with one word before moving to the next one. In picking random words, the emphasis should be in using them **spontaneously**.

Generate and write down all the ideas as quickly as you can in the initial "brainstorming" stage. There is no one "right way" to use a random word. Any and every way is right, as long as movement of the mind is happening.

Within a group of people, there will be several completely different uses of the same random word in the same problem setting. The group environment can supercharge the process, as long as each participant is allowed to contribute without embarrassment or ridicule. However, the main advantage of REST is that ONE PERSON can use it quite effectively in his own privacy, at any time.

If you make a habit of spending just ten to fifteen minutes a day applying the REST to any real or practice problem, the development of your creative thinking skills will be rapidly improved.

The main point with the REST is that of acquiring confidence.

At first, it might seem incredible that a truly random word could have any use at all. The course of action is totally opposite to traditional, analytical procedures, which seek only the relevant and essential. However, when you understand how the mind works, it is impossible for any external stimulus to remain irrelevant. Your confidence grows as you become more familiar with the process.

Random external stimulation depends on the patterning nature of the mind for its strong effect. The random word can open up a new entry point and change that entry point completely.

Referred to as Lateral thinking, this is one of the most powerful ways of modifying a problem. A new entry point means that the old pattern is entered from a new position and it could lead you to a new choice

Random external stimulation has many advantages:

• It takes little time.

• You could work with it on your own.

• It is a deliberate process as opposed to waiting for something to happen.

• It ignites the synthetic and creative imagination processes.

• It is effective for everyone regardless of education occupation, age, or sex.

• It is unique.

• It is easy to master.

• It is practical compared to long winded cumbersome and complicated theories.

• It is personally rewarding

• It is fun to do

• It will always produce results.

How Random Words Work

If we would describe the Random External Stimulus Technique in other words, we could call it the RANDOM WORD STIMULATOR. That is exactly what the REST does. It stimulates the mind by the input of random words, and it makes a strong impact upon the conscious and subconscious mind.

One of the strongest aspects of this system is having an endless supply of random rather than selected words. The words used must be unexpected, uncalled for, completely independent one from another, and show themselves by absolute randomness BY CHANCE.

We know from previous chapters that the majority of inventions and discoveries have happened by chance or happy accident. REST creates chance inputs at will. It enables us to utilize this strange faculty of the mind, without waiting long periods for a "Eureka", or "AHA" moment, as some people call it.

The chance happenings and happy accidents are now within your grasp. Just point (or click it you have downloaded ThinkTank SFI for a WORD, and chance appears almost instantly. All you have to do is connect the words you see with your mental engine and presto, you get a fast link in a long chain of associations, which will move your mind in unexpected and unpredictable directions. Every proper word (nouns are best) in the English language can and will produce all kinds of thoughts in your mind.

From previous chapters, you have gained some experience for the association of ideas triggered by a single word. Those associations were simply a demonstration of the imagination process of the mind. They merely serve as a means of illustrating about this marvellous ability of the mind to move by linking up one thought to another and another to infinity. That link-up will have some structure, some purposeful meaning, and direction.

What do we do? We simply take a word, ANY WORD, and connect its meaning to a structured thought. For example, you sit home bored and restless. You want to do something, or go somewhere, but you have no idea what and where.

You randomly found these words:
RIPPLE, MANEKIN, FILIBUSTER.

As you see, these words have nothing in common, either with your problem or with each other. Most likely, you would never put these three words together, even if you find three unrelated words on your own.

They are as different as any three words could be. Now consider these words, one at a time, together with your problem, and see what new trains of thought would occur in your mind. You will use your mind to force the meaning, and the association of a given word, or sets of words, to a problem. If we want to see where these words will lead us, we will simply gather assorted ideas.

This is the first STAGE OF THINKING, the imagination stage as explained previously. Before deciding what action to take, let us examine all of them and eventually come to a definite conclusion as to which of these ideas will appeal to us.

This is the processing stage, the logical stage of implementation of a chosen idea.

Once we make the choice, we are ready to proceed with ACTION. We move ahead with all necessary steps to see how our chosen idea would work.

Now, let us see how this would work in practice. Back to

your problem and to our previous situation.

You are home, bored and restless. You want to do something or go somewhere, but you have no idea what and where.

How do you use the three words: RIPPLE, MANEKIN, FILIBUSTER?

Use one word at the time, and list as many thoughts as your own associative process will allow you, keeping in mind your selected problem.

Your thinking may go like this:

RIPPLE - widening circles when I throw a stone into a placid pond. Widening circles remind me of widening circle of friends.

The idea: set up one new goal to find one new friend today, to widen my circle of friends. The pond reminds me of the swimming pool at YMCA. An idea: go to YMCA, have a swim, and make one new friend today.

MANEKIN doll, display windows, stores, store browsing, window-shopping. Here is an idea: go window-shopping with a purpose. The purpose could be to choose the best displayed MANEKIN, giving marks to each, and then award the store with the best Manekin display by looking to make a purchase.

Spend a few hours and choose MISS MANEKIN.

This would be a good way of passing time.

FILIBUSTER- The obstruction of the process in the legislature, Parliament, and public gallery.

An idea: go to the Parliament building, and listen to the proceedings, listen to the representatives of the government, and to those of the opposition.

The thought about my presence in public gallery leads me to the thought about court proceedings. I have never been to one. How about going to the criminal court and listening to the real-life dramas? Here you have several ideas, which came to your mind by a chain of association triggered by a single word. In all probability, you would have not come up with similar ideas on your own; otherwise, you would not have been bored in the first place. Your mind moves from a static position to several paths, which you could follow.

This FIRST STAGE OF THINKING serves as a method of gathering numerous ideas, many alternatives, and many paths. You should accumulate ideas before you decide on one to take action. When a sufficient number of ideas are available, look them over and apply your JUDGEMENT as to which one appeals to you the most. Once you make a choice, act upon it.

Go ahead and pass into the SECOND STAGE OF THINKING, the stage of idea implementation.

The above example is simple and light-hearted; it serves as an elementary explanation of the REST. We have taken three words only for the purpose of simplification, but you could continue and work on other words, and get larger number of ideas and broader choices.

In this demonstration, we have generated only two ideas from each word giving us six choices. Actually, we could multiply this process many folds and generate ten or more ideas from each word. Some of them might be good, some might make sense, and others could be not serious or even feasible.

That is not important.

What matters here is to utilize the elasticity of your mind, and move it in many directions, gathering speed as you go, regardless if along the way you pick up some foolish ideas. Remember: silly ideas could become stepping-stones to great ideas.

In your lesson, NEW THINK, you have learned that "nonsense" could make a lot of sense when you apply your IMAGINATION. The same would be valid here. In this case, you act on a specific problem. You generate new thoughts using a single word as a starting point, extracting an association from a word, and forcing that association on your problem. In other words, you accomplish a connection where there was none. Your connections between a word and a plausible idea are, in brief, the essence of Lateral Thinking.

You will have many opportunities to work on more complex problem situations and learn about many other uses for

REST. You will have many questions pertaining to the ways of using the random word method.

I designed this guide to answer all of your questions, if not in a direct way, then by way of many examples and EXERCISE ACTIVITIES. They form the best and the most important part of your development.

I believe the best method of learning is by doing, repeatedly, until the whole process becomes as familiar to you as the alphabet.

FREQUENTLY ASKED QUESTIONS

HOW MANY WORDS SHOULD I USE? You can use any number of words. You can use as many as you like. A word of caution: totally exhaust a word before moving to the next. If you easily give up and change a word when the going gets a little tough, you may develop the habit of moving on too easily. Use a smaller number of words, perhaps two, three or four and run with them.

WHICH WORDS SHOULD I USE? Use any word, which you can clearly understand the meaning of. If you have Think Tank SFI the definitions of every word are provided.

This is a very important point. Sometimes, you may not like a certain word, and you will tend to want to pass it over, looking for a "better" one. There is no such a thing as the "better" word. If you are looking for it, you are consciously trying to come up with new ideas by a logical process.

By selecting a word or words with your logical thinking, you destroy the valuable method of randomness the vital strength of the REST.

The Random Word method works better, when less similarity exists between a word and a specific task. The more dissimilar the two are, the more likely is that the chance input will trigger original ideas. Some words may seem trivial, but you may be surprised that some "trivial" words can and often do contain a wealth of useful ideas.

ADJECTIVES, VERBS, OR NOUNS? From extensive testing and experience, I have concluded that the nouns facilitate the production of associations better than adjectives.

Think Tank SFI includes many verbs, which suggest action. They are most effective for the DIRECT use of a word. A word could become a command, an order to do something specific.

Many words in the English language have the same or similar meaning, understanding the meanings and use of these words, especially those words that have stronger psychological impact will be of great benefit to the process.

QUESTION: INSTEAD OF THINK TANK SFI,
CAN I USE A DICTIONARY?

Yes, you can, except for several disadvantages. Any instrument or tool could be a substitute for something else less effective and more primitive. Why use a hammer when a stone could do the job? Why use the car to go to New

York, when you could go on foot, or with horse and buggy? Why use an electric kettle, when you could boil water in a pot? Why use the printing press, when you could write the same text by hand?

The following are the principal reasons why a dictionary is not satisfactory. Using the dictionary would be a primitive tool compared to Think Tank SFI.

1. Selecting the random words guarantees their strong psychological value.

2. A dictionary does not provide total RANDOMNESS.

3. Using a dictionary, you dissipate your attention as you are likely to apply the next word that you see, or a derivative of the same word, which has poor value for associations.

4. It is very difficult to point to an exact word in the dictionary. You may be required to "pick" a word above, below or beside where your finger landed, thereby losing some of the randomness.

5. Think Tank SFI provides random words INSTANTLY, the dictionary does not.

6. Think Tank SFI creates the endless possibility of obtaining totally unrelated words instantly, at a click of a button.

7. Think Tank SFI does for new ideas what an electronic calculator does for mathematics. It is PRACTICAL, FAST,

and EFFICIENT.

WHAT IS IN A WORD?

There are four different ways of using individual words.

They are:

A. ASSOCIATIONS

B. FUNCTIONS.

C. DIRECT

D. PUN or HUMOUR

ASSOCIATIONS: We have previously dealt with the subject of associations. No need to repeat it here.

FUNCTIONS: Almost every word contains some sort of function that could be extremely important for the applications in the RWT system. For example: Let us use the word CURTAIN. What type of function could we extract from it?

CURTAIN: Protection. Curtain protects the interior of the house from the harmful effects of the sun.

CURTAIN: Privacy. Creates the privacy by blocking the inside view from outside passersby.

CURTAIN: It provides the shading. CURTAIN: It hangs on small hooks that are connected to rollers that roll on a metal or plastic rod. This function could be the solution to an engineering product that would have escaped the sharp mind of a technician. DIRECT. This is a way that the word, which appears from the RWT, commands the user to do something so obvious that the user never considered. It is almost like an awakening, a mental shock, an electric blitz. For example, let us use the following words: BEND, CRACK, STICK, HEAT, WRITE, GIVE, REPEAT etc.

PUN: Humor, or Jibe, or Wisecrack, or Joke. A word could hide or contain any of these meanings. The fact is that humor is a great provoker of creativity. When you are in good mood, you laugh at any silly joke. Your mind is in a state of relaxation and ideas pop up very quickly.

Relaxed mind is the promoter of good, imaginative, creative, inventive, thinking. Here are some examples: WOOD: Mood, Crack, Orphan, Leafy, Spiffy etc.

As you see a word, any word regardless how unimportant it might seem, could be a great starting point for new and imaginative ideas. Please appreciate any and all of them and apply one of the four ways of extracting ideas from them. It is not important which of the four ways you apply to a given word.

There is no special order here; it is rather like your mind: imaginative, inventive, creative, resourceful, innovative.

MORE FREQUENTLY ASKED QUESTIONS

SHOULD I USE THE RES ALONE? Not necessarily. In your lesson "Group Brainstorming", we explained how this method could and should be used in group sessions in the company of family members or friends. You could also use it as a social game. However, for serious work and serious stimulation of ideas in YOUR mind, it is the best to work alone in an atmosphere of relaxation and peacefulness.

WHEN IS THE BEST TIME TO WORK WITH RES? It depends on your personal preferences. The best time is when your mind is in a state of repose, when you feel light and easy, when you do not wrestle with any business or domestic problems, when your thoughts are the clearest. For some people this would mean early morning, for others late at night.

HOW OFTEN SHOULD I PRACTICE? You could work your mind any time you wish and spend as much time as you like. I promote the regular practice; a good idea is to set aside several minutes every day for REST activity, especially if your mind is at ease, and when you have nothing of importance to do. If you need new ideas, fresh insights, and creative thoughts, embrace the REST; it will stimulate you for greatness.

You should isolate yourself and work alone, as long as you need to come up with a useful idea or ideas. It may take you an hour to gather ideas and alternatives, until you are satisfied that you could implement one or several of them.

The more you use RES, the more effective, and realizable it will be for you.

CAN ANYBODY USE REST? Yes, regardless of one's profession, occupation, intellectual standing, age or sex. REST utilizes the most natural, and the most automatic attributes of the mind — free associations — and each rational person uses the free associations every day, and every hour of their consciousness.

We strongly recommend the encouragement for the use of REST by CHILDREN, AFTER THEY LEARN HOW TO READ AND WRITE.

The children are much more creative than adults are because their minds do not toy with old ideas and old concepts. Since the schools do not encourage the development of the natural creativeness of children, RES could help greatly.

This program fascinates most children. You could give them just a basic idea how to use it and they will go at it with interest and enthusiasm.

WHAT TO DO WITH THE UNFAMILIAR WORDS? There are some words, which might not be familiar to you. You should use such words for two reasons:

1. By using these words you learn and enrich your vocabulary.

2. By learning the meaning of unfamiliar words, you could

use it for REST processes and free associations. This will help you to retain such words in your memory forever.

From our previous experience with ideas and people, we have learned that when it comes to undertaking a new approach, a new path, a new way of looking at problems, this becomes a puzzle for many individuals. After all, they possess the marvellous engine located in their skull, their brains.

They have great difficulty to break out of the well-established system of patterns that is crowding their minds.

BE CLEAR ABOUT THE PROBLEM

Since they are unable to think creatively, the degrees of getting new ideas, their creative quotient approaches the point near zero. We have known this for a long time. In countless occasions, people with all kinds of problems, were unable to solve them. Some of these problems involved their personal and family lives, some were of technical nature, and others dealt with social and political matters. It is amazing how the majority of regular individuals do not know how to do the following:

1. Define clearly their problems. Sometimes a clear and intelligent definition of a problem helps to solve it.

2. Simplify a problem and reduce it to its basic components, so that you can see it better and clearer.

3. Find a solution, which is so obvious at times, that you do not see it. To many people the obvious solution is far away, because they could not conceive the thought that sometimes the most obvious solution is the best one. Perhaps they think the obvious solution is too simple to be of any use.

4. Detach yourself from a problem, and look at it from a little distance, from an impartial point of view, and exclude personal emotions.

5. Use a little imagination, which is in great abundance in the mind of every normal person. The people need to unlock their minds and allow their thoughts to flow naturally.

Through the years, some people have developed a habit of finding unusual solutions to usual problems using Lateral Thinking. In some cases, it was a matter of life and death.

On a number of occasions, people had to take an unusual approach to save their life, especially in times of war.

Here is an example of identifying the problem:

"I want to quit my Job."

"If that is your problem, the solution is easy. Just quit."

"Yes, but I want another job, and I do not have one lined up."

Why do you want to quit?",

"I don't like my job"

This person does not KNOW what the real problem is. He/She did not define the problem clearly.

The conversation can continue: "I have worked at the same job in the same place for the last seven years. The job is boring, the pay is not bad, but the work does not provide any satisfaction to me."

"So, your problem is not that you want to quit your job; your problem could be defined this way: Find a new job, which will be pleasant, and pay about the same amount of money as I am getting now. The fact that you want to abandon the present job for another one, is just one of the steps you must undertake to find a good solution to your problem."

This kind of discussion prompts one to start thinking about ways of nudging to become a genuine source of powerful ideas. We know the equipment is there, in the head of every rational person. The question is how to free that power and harness it for useful and productive purposes.

Our thinking went like this: If we take a thought, imagine it to be one single kernel of grain, then multiply it by the power of 2, Example: 1 - 2 - 4 - 8 - 16 etc., doubling the last sum to infinity, what would happen? After a longish calculation, it was clear to us that we would use up all the grain in existence everywhere in the world, and reach that quantity starting from one solitary kernel!

There is a limit to the number of grain kernels, but there is no limit to the quantity of thoughts. If we reverse this analogy and change the kernel of grain into the thought, it would confirm that creative thinking has no limit.

This kind of speculative thinking or philosophizing was going on in our minds and we could not free ourselves from it. Many other ideas raced through our brainpower in an endless chain. Some of them reminded us of the force of a hurricane, some sailed quietly on a placid lake, and others had a touch of madness.

Why not take one of those antiquated dictionaries, cut out individual words, spread them on a table and allow their randomness to act as triggers to the mind, so that the mind could come up with new and different ideas?

Of course, you should remember that the "new and different ideas" do not occur unless you unlock and open your mind for them. When they come in, a meaningful outcome may also come. We already thought about some method for the stimulation of the mind, and its power for creative ideas, by using all those words, spread out on the table, for some practical idea-producing device. Remember, that chance favours the prepared mind.

We have now prepared our minds and opened its gates for new possibilities. From the previous pages, the most brilliant ideas and inventions are beautifully simple.

However, it is not easy to simplify things, we know that. We also know that the mind works easier when it travels the roads paved with complications. The mind, for some unexplained reasons, tends to complicate things rather than simplify them.

Unless we undertake a DELIBERATE effort to simplify a problem, we hurry and burden it with countless side matters and unimportant details.

For Further Development and
Advanced Techniques please visit
www.LateralThinkingCourse.com

ISBN-14: 978-0-9879184-0-6

www.ingramcontent.com/pod-product-compliance
Lightning Source LLC
Chambersburg PA
CBHW060633290526
45793CB00001B/227